THE
GARLIC LOVERS
COOKBOOK
VOLUME II

©1979 G.G.F.A. Inc.

FROM GILROY, CALIFORNIA
GARLIC CAPITAL OF THE WORLD

CELESTIAL ARTS
Berkeley

Copyright © 1985, 2005 by the Gilroy Garlic Festival. All rights reserved. Published in the United States by Celestial Arts, an imprint of the Crown Publishing Group, a division of Random House, Inc., New York.
www.crownpublishing.com
www.tenspeed.com

Celestial Arts and the Celestial Arts colophon are registered trademarks of Random House, Inc.

Library of Congress Cataloging-in-Publication Data is on file with the publisher.

ISBN 10: 1-58761-237-2
ISBN 13: 978-1-58761-237-4

Printed in the United States of America

Cover design: Toni Tajima
Cover photograph: Diane Padys, Taxi/Getty Images
Interior design: Chloe Rawlins
Interior illustrations: Nancy Austin

13 12 11 10 9 8 7 6 5 4
Revised Edition

ACKNOWLEDGMENTS

In keeping with the spirit of the Gilroy Garlic Festival, the *Garlic Lovers' Cookbook, Volume II* was made possible through sharing and volunteerism.

It began with the creative entrants in the Great Garlic Recipe Contest and Cook-off who shared their treasured recipes. Then the volunteers devoted themselves to the task of reading, examining and classifying each recipe. The selection process was also one of sharing as the volunteer cooks chose and prepared the dishes for their families and friends to taste and critique.

The Gilroy Garlic Festival wishes to express special gratitude to these generous individuals whose contributions have made it possible to publish the *Garlic Lovers' Cookbook, Volume II*. Special thanks, also, to Karen Christopher, Garlic Lovers' Cookbook Coordinator, and Caryl Saunders Associates for their professional input.

Without the generosity of so many people, this book and its predecessor, the *Garlic Lovers' Cookbook*, would not be nearly as interesting nor inclusive of so many great ideas for cooking with garlic—and with love.

Garlic Festival Association
P.O. Box 2311
Gilroy, California 95021
(408) 842-1625
www.gilroygarlicfestival.com

Contents

THE PEOPLE OF GILROY

The first reviews were great: "The ultimate in summer food fairs." *(Los Angeles Herald Examiner);* "Fame is nothing to sniff at in Gilroy." *(Washington Post);* "It was rollicking good fun and the food was super." *(San Francisco Chronicle);* "By any measure, it was a success." *(San Francisco Examiner).* The nationwide headlines, proclaiming the phenomenal success of the first Garlic Festival in 1979 caught the people of Gilroy by surprise.

When a group of local residents staged the first weekend celebration of the "scented pearl" to increase community pride and help create a more flavorable image of their town, little did they know what a dramatic impact it would make on Gilroy. What they did know was how to use the area's most prominent product, garlic. They knew how to cook up cauldrons of mouthwatering garlic-laced food, how to have fun with garlic, how to motivate people and how to share this very special lifestyle. The rest is history and the Garlic Festival became a permanent fixture on the town calendar.

Garlic now gives the town (Gilroy) a certain dignity...

–Wall Street Journal

The response to Gilroy's harvest festival surpassed even the most optimistic expectations. Yearly attendance grew from 20,000 to 120,000 and by 1985 over half a million visitors had trekked to Gilroy, "The Garlic Capital of the World," to share in the culinary legacy of its residents.

The steering committee of community leaders, determined to provide a quality event, rose to meet the challenges created by the ever-increasing numbers of garlic lovers: More garlic! More space! More food! More planning! More volunteers! All this, and a more enviable challenge: Determine the best use for the monies generated at each year's event.

More garlic? No problem in Gilroy. More space? Solved with cooperation from the city's award-winning Parks Department and the generosity of local landowners. To meet the other needs a cross section of Gilroy residents formed thirty committees to deal with the creative aspects, detailed planning, logistics, and implementation of each phase of the festival. The Gilroy Garlic Festival Association was formed as a nonprofit, tax-exempt private corporation with a rotating board of directors. The Association's continuing goal was identified as the support of community projects, charitable groups and service organizations. Several criteria were established for the disbursement of Festival funds, but the majority of funds available is given to those groups who have directly participated in the event through commitment of time and labor. (Voila! More volunteers.) Additional monies are used for permanent improvements to Gilroy's parks for all to enjoy.

From 1979 to 1984 the yearly volunteer base of the Festival grew from 50 to 4,000; participating organizations from 15 to 115; man-hours contributed increased from a few hundred to 33,000; and yearly distributed monies increased from $5,500 to $250,000.

The festival of harvest is, of course, a unifying event as old as civilization itself, but to do it well is the equivalent of staging an opera or anything else that lifts the spirit. In this regard, Gilroy is approaching the first rank.

—*San Francisco Examiner*

In the light of these extraordinary facts, the media headlines took on new meaning. "Gilroy provided an experience to warm the heart." *(San Francisco Examiner);* "Garlic now gives the town (Gilroy) a certain dignity." *(Wall Street Journal);* "Enjoy a town being proud of itself and transforming the pungent aroma of garlic into the sweet smell of success." *(The Urban Fair,* U.S. Department, HUD); "Garlic breathes new life into town." *(Washington Post)* In reality, garlic is simply the product and the Garlic Festival is the vehicle for people to help themselves and each other.

Volunteers are matched to their Festival job by skill level, ability, and willingness to eagerly give hours to help the charity or organization of their choice, including hospitals, libraries, rape crisis centers, battered women's shelters, drug abuse prevention programs, sports and service clubs, rehabilitation facilities for the handicapped, plus local, senior citizen, school, church, and cultural groups, as well as for the better known national organizations such as the American Cancer Society, American Heart Association, American Red Cross, and Special Olympics—110 organizations in all.

But are the dollars the only motivation for helping? The following testimonials, from Festival volunteers, are the ones we are most proud off:

"It is a convergence of good. It is neighbors helping
neighbors in a celebration of our community."
—*Albert Valencia, South County Alternative, Inc.*

"Working together to create an event we are all proud
of is worth so much more than the financial returns."
—*Richard Imler, Gilroy High School*

"A time when community spirit unites and
takes precedence over all other activities."
—*Karen Rizzi, Children's Home Society*

"The Festival is the epitome of people giving and
sharing of themselves for a common cause."
—*Oscar Torres, Jr., Big Brothers/Big Sisters*

So in reality it is not only Gilroy's famous garlic but Gilroy's main resource—its people—that guarantees an enjoyable time for all who visit the Festival.

THE FESTIVAL

Whether you appreciate garlic for its flavor, its health aspects or its folklore, you'll want to travel to Gilroy and experience the annual Garlic Festival. The ultimate in summer food fairs, the Gilroy Garlic Festival features a truly international array of epicurean garlic delights. Gourmet Alley is the heart of this food showcase, where local chefs perform culinary magic over the fire pits in full view of spectators. These wizards work wonders with iron skillets the size of bicycle wheels as they toss the flaming calamari or gently sauté bright red and green peppers. Mouthwatering mountains of garlic bread, tons of scampi swimming in lobster butter sauce, delicate stuffed mushrooms, cauldrons of pasta con pesto, and slabs of sirloin basted in garlic marinade set the standards for quality and adherence to the garlic theme that prevails.

Eighty additional food booths operated by service clubs, civic and merchant groups offer a breathtaking variety of garlic creations. After sampling the aromatic offerings of the talented townspeople of Gilroy, visitors can cool their palates with the local wines, a cold drink, or garlic ice cream and desserts of local fresh fruits.

The festival, which celebrates the end of this year's garlic harvest, really is small-town America at its best.

*—Keith Muroaka,
The [Santa Cruz] Sentinel*

Mr. Garlic and Miss Gilroy Garlic Festival reign over the festivities. Visitors will find all kinds of garlic, including fresh bulbs (pee-wee to colossal sizes), garlic braids and garlands, dry decorative arrangements, all forms of dehydrated and processed garlic, garlic-themed cookbooks, information on garlic's medicinal and health uses, garlic folklore, plus hats, t-shirts, jewelry, and more. Guests can also make their own garlic braids and watch garlic "topping" demonstrations (a harvesting technique that removes the tops and roots with sharp shears).

At the Arts and Crafts area, over 100 booths of juried fine arts and crafts feature many original works, including some garlic-themed creations. Musicians and strolling entertainers perform continuously. Added to these ingredients is a generous dash of small-town conviviality, and the result is a recipe for a truly unique summer experience whose savory memories will be with you even longer than the lingering smell of garlic.

People flocked to this little farming community 80 miles south of San Francisco. When the crowds weren't eating, they were singing garlic songs, swapping garlic seeds and recipes... buying garlic souvenirs.

—*Christian Science Monitor*

THE GILROY GARLIC FESTIVAL RECIPE CONTEST

The Garlic Recipe Contest, held each year in connection with the Gilroy Garlic Festival, was originally intended to be a wonderful adventure in garlic cooking rather than a commercial enterprise. Because the Festival's primary purpose is to support local charities, it was decided to keep the prizes relatively small so that more of the proceeds from the festival could be contributed to philanthropic organizations. Entrants who qualify for the final Cook-off are expected to bring their own pots, pans, and ingredients. One might think these conditions would discourage participants, but such is not the case. Nearly 1,000 entries pour in every year from garlic lovers throughout the United States who want to share their great garlic cooking discoveries with others who will truly appreciate them.

The bulb's biggest booster since King Tut.

—People Magazine

Contest rules specify that recipes must call for a minimum of 6 cloves of fresh garlic or the equivalent in dehydrated or processed garlic. Recipes must be original, and only amateur chefs are permitted to enter the Contest. When recipes are received at the Festival office, the volunteer committee chairman and committee members cull those that do not meet Contest requirements.

The recipes that qualify are sent to a select group of professional home economists in San Francisco who themselves are in the business of developing new recipes for food clients and who understand all the problems related to such endeavors. They carefully read and compare recipes, searching for the unusual technique or combination of ingredients that might make a particular recipe a winner. Recipes are prepared exactly as specified by the entrant and then taste-tested. When the prejudging is done, the finalists are notified and invited to participate in the Cook-off where the winners will be selected.

Judges who serve at the Cook-off are chosen from the professional food world for their knowledge and expertise. Many have judged the most important cooking contests in the country, yet all agree that the Garlic Recipe Contest is the most fun.

All recipes entered in the Contest become the property of the Gilroy Garlic Festival Association, and it is with this wonderful collection that the *Garlic Lovers' Cookbook (Volumes I and II)* began.

Garlic is more than a fad. It's a phenomenon.

—Chicago Sun-Times

Each recipe entry is filed by category and made available to community members for testing in their own kitchens. Evaluation forms are provided which include information as to number of servings, ease of cooking, ease of obtaining ingredients, clarity of directions, and visual appeal. Most important are freelance comments. There's no mistaking: "Yuck! I wouldn't serve this to my dog" or "My family loved it" or "Our absolute favorite."

Add only the best from these tested recipes to the winners and finalists from previous years and the *Garlic Lovers' Cookbook* represents a rare collection indeed.

KNOW YOUR GARLIC

Fresh garlic may be creamy white or have a purplish-red cast, but whatever the color, it should be plump and firm, with its papery covering intact, not spongy, soft, or shriveled. Dehydrated or other forms of processed garlic should be purchased in tightly sealed containers.

Storage

Fresh garlic keeps best in a cool, dry place with plenty of ventilation. It should not be refrigerated unless you separate the cloves and immerse them in oil, either peeled or unpeeled. If the garlic isn't peeled, the cloves will hold their firmness longer, but peeling later will be more difficult. Fresh garlic that is held in open-air storage for any length of time will lose some of its pungency and may even develop sprouts. The garlic is still usable, but will be somewhat milder and more will be needed to achieve the same strength of flavor.

Dehydrated forms of garlic should be stored with other spices in as cool and dry a place as possible, definitely not above or next to a kitchen range, sink, or in front of a window with exposure to the sun. Keep tightly sealed. Processed garlic, which requires refrigeration after opening, should, of course, always be stored in the refrigerator to maintain quality.

Peeling

When peeling only a few cloves, simply press each clove against the cutting board with the flat side of a heavy kitchen knife, or press the clove between the thumbs and forefinger to loosen the skin first. If a recipe calls for a large quantity of garlic, drop the cloves in boiling water for just a minute and drain quickly. They will peel quite easily. If you have a microwave oven, you can cook the cloves for 5 seconds or so to achieve the same effect.

You can cook unpeeled garlic in a hot pan (it doesn't burn easily), then slip off the skins when the garlic is soft. Or, if the garlic is to be cooked in a soup or sauce and with the whole cloves discarded later, there is no need to peel them. And, if you are preparing a dish such as "Thirty Clove Chicken," cook the cloves unpeeled and then simply press the soft garlic out of the skin with your fingers or with a knife and fork as you eat it.

Is Fresh Always Best?

Whether you use fresh, dehydrated, or processed garlic is a matter of personal choice. Fresh garlic fans note that garlic flavors food differently, depending on how it is used. Fresh uncooked garlic is most pungent when puréed, crushed, or finely minced. For milder garlic flavor, keep the cloves whole or cut into large pieces. Whole cloves cooked for a long time with roasts, stews, or soups have a surprisingly sweet, nutlike flavor. It is very important when cooking with fresh garlic *not* to burn it. When garlic is burned, it produces a very bitter flavor and must be discarded or it will ruin the dish. Remember, when sautéing garlic in oil, keep the heat fairly low and cook it until it is just very lightly browned.

Other forms of garlic vary somewhat in their flavoring characteristics, but you can generally plan on the following substitutions:

1 average-sized clove of garlic =

⅛ teaspoon dehydrated, powdered, minced, or chopped garlic

or

½ teaspoon garlic salt. (*Caution:* when using garlic salt in recipes calling for fresh garlic, decrease the amount of salt called for.)

The Pungent Herb

Several techniques help to control the odor of garlic on the hands that results from peeling or chopping. Disposable plastic gloves can be worn while performing this chore. Or you can rub the fingers with salt and lemon juice afterward, then rinse under cold water. The best solution we've found is to rub the fingers over the bowl of a stainless steel teaspoon under running water for a few moments. There is a chemical reaction that takes place that does indeed eliminate the odor from the skin. The more garlic chopped, the longer it will take to remove the aroma.

Garlic odor on the breath is most easily controlled by eating fresh parsley. Parsley has been called "nature's mouthwash" by garlic lovers because of its effectiveness. Chewing on a coffee bean or two also seems to do the trick.

To Chop or Press?

Some chefs swear by their garlic presses and others claim that using a garlic press makes the fresh garlic taste bitter. It is certainly a quick and easy method of mincing garlic; however, you do lose some of the pulp which means that hand-chopped gives a better yield and less waste. Again, the choice is yours. If you choose to chop by hand, here's a tip from the wife of a garlic grower: Add the salt required for your recipe directly into the minced garlic while it is still on the cutting board. The salt will absorb the juices and make it easier to scoop the tiny garlic pieces off the board.

Flavored Oil, Vinegar, and Salt

It's easy to flavor seasonings by adding peeled whole garlic cloves to bottles of oil or vinegar for two or three days before using. To make garlic salt, just bury 3 peeled and pressed garlic cloves in $1/2$ cup of salt. Add fresh ground pepper and ground ginger to taste, if you like. Let stand for a few days in a screw-top jar. Remove garlic and use the salt as desired to flavor soups, meats, and salads.

Garlic Butter

Make logs of garlic butter and freeze them to have on hand to melt on broiled meats or to mix into fresh cooked vegetables or spread on bread. Just add mashed garlic cloves, or the equivalent in dehydrated or processed garlic, to suit your taste to sticks of butter (about 6 cloves fresh garlic per stick is recommended). If you wish, add a few herbs and salt lightly. Form into logs, wrap in plastic, and freeze. Slice off as needed.

Baked Garlic Heads

One of the most popular ways to serve fresh garlic is to bake whole heads to serve as an hors d'oeuvre with crunchy bread or as an accompaniment to meat or vegetables. Peel as much of the outer skin away as possible, leaving the cloves unpeeled and the head intact. Place heads in a covered casserole or on a piece of heavy aluminum foil, drizzle with olive oil, dot with butter, salt and pepper to taste, and bake, covered, at 350 degrees F. for about 45 minutes or until cloves are soft and can be squeezed easily out of their skins onto bread or other foods.

Special Terms

Bulb The name for the usable portion of fresh garlic made up of as many as 15 or more individual cloves.

Clove One of several segments of a bulb, each of which is covered with a thin, papery skin.

Crushed A term that refers to fresh garlic that has been smashed by the broad side of a knife or cleaver on a chopping board or with a rolling pin between several sheets of waxed paper.

Dehydrated Any of several forms of garlic from which the moisture has been removed. Dehydrated garlic is available minced, powdered, and granulated.

Fresh The term used to describe garlic that has not been dehydrated. Actually "fresh" garlic is allowed to "cure" in the field before harvesting just until the papery skin, not the cloves, become dry.

Garlic Braid A garland of fresh garlic braided together by its tops. Braiding is done while the garlic is still only partially cured with some moisture remaining in the fibers and before the tops are removed in harvesting. When they become fully dried, they are too brittle to handle easily. Originally devised as a convenient storage method, they are quite decorative. Serious garlic lovers like to use them for cooking purposes, cutting off one bulb at a time. Care should be taken if the braid is to be preserved as a decoration that it is not handled carelessly. The papery covering on the bulbs is fragile and will flake and tear easily when the garlic itself has shriveled after a year or so.

Garlic is enveloping the country.

–Twin Falls Idaho Times News

Granulated A dehydrated form of garlic that is five times stronger than raw garlic. Its flavor is released only in the presence of moisture.

Juice Garlic juice may be purchased commercially or prepared by squeezing fresh cloves in a garlic press, being certain not to include any of the flesh. Juice blends easily for uniform flavor.

Minced This term is used for both dehydrated and fresh garlic. It's generally called for when small pieces of garlic are desirable, as in soups, sauces, or salad dressings. Fresh garlic may be minced using a sharp knife on a chopping board. If the recipe calls for salt, add it to the garlic while mincing. It will prevent the garlic from sticking to the knife and absorb the juices otherwise lost in the mincing process. Finely minced garlic, as called for in most French recipes, tends to disappear into the finished dish. For a more robust flavor, mince more coarsely as called for in many Chinese dishes. Large amounts of garlic can be minced using a blender or food processor.

Powdered Powdered garlic is available commercially. When using powder in recipes with a high acid content, mix with water (2 parts water to 1 part powder) before adding. Powdered garlic can be made from fresh by slowing drying peeled garlic cloves in the oven. When very dry, pound or crush until fine and powdery. Pass through a sieve and pound any large pieces, then sieve again. Store in sealed jars in a dry place.

No one is indifferent to garlic. People either love it or hate it, and most good cooks seem to belong in the first group.

—*Los Angeles Herald Examiner*

Pressed A term for garlic that has been put through a garlic press. There are many different types of presses available, some even "self-cleaning." When using a press, it isn't necessary to peel the garlic clove. Simply cut it in half and place in the press. Then squeeze. The skin will stay behind, making the press easier to clean. Remember to clean a press immediately after use before the small particles that remain have a chance to dry.

Purée A term for garlic that has been cooked at high heat and then pressed through a sieve. It's available commercially or made at home. It is excellent to have on hand to blend into soups, sauces, or to spread on slices of bread to serve with hors d'oeuvres.

Garlic Salt Available commercially, it is usually a blend of approximately 90% salt, approximately 9% garlic, and approximately 1% free-flowing agent. When using garlic salt in recipes calling for fresh garlic, decrease the amount of salt called for.

Cooking Equivalents Table

Kitchen Measure

3 teaspoons = 1 tablespoon
2 tablespoons = 1 fluid ounce
16 tablespoons = 1 cup
8 ounces = 1 cup or ½ pound
16 ounces = 1 pound
2 cups = 1 pint
2 pints = 1 quart
4 pints = 2 quarts or ½ gallon
8 pints = 4 quarts or 1 gallon
4 quarts = 1 gallon

Metric Measure

1 ounce = 28.55 grams
1 gram = .035 ounce
8 ounces = 226.78 grams or ½ pound
100 grams = 3½ ounces
500 grams = 1 pound (generous)
1 pound = ½ kilogram (scant)
1 kilogram = 2¼ pounds (scant)
⅒ liter = ½ cup (scant) or ¼ pint (scant)
½ liter = 2 cups (generous) or 1 pint (generous)
1 quart = 1 liter (scant, or .9463 liter)
1 liter = 1 quart (generous, or 1.0567 quarts)
1 liter = 4½ cups or 1 quart 2 ounces
1 gallon = 3.785 liters (approximately 3¾ liters)

APPETIZERS AND SNACKS

ROASTED GARLIC PURÉE DIP

This is a truly versatile recipe. The purée can be used on cooked vegetables, fish, steaks, salad greens, or baked potatoes. You can double the recipe if you want to keep some on hand.

Best Recipe Using the Most Garlic Winner 1984 Recipe Contest: **Mary Fencl, Forestdale, MA**

6 large heads (about 72 cloves) fresh garlic

4 ounces blue cheese, at room temperature

¾ cup milk

2 tablespoons chopped fresh parsley

Crudités (assorted fresh, raw vegetables, sliced for dipping)

Remove outer cover on garlic. Do not peel or separate the cloves. Place each garlic head on a large square of heavy aluminum foil. Fold up the foil so the cloves are completely wrapped. Bake for 1 hour at 350 degrees F. Remove garlic from the oven and cool for 10 minutes. Separate and squeeze cloves to remove cooked garlic. Discard skins. In a food processor, combine cheeses, milk and garlic, and process until smooth. Place in a serving dish and sprinkle with parsley. Serve as a dip with crudités for dipping.

Makes about 5 cups.

APHRA DE JACQUES

This prize-winning cook named her recipe to approximate the word "aphrodisiac," because her husband claimed eating it made him amorous. Who knows? Legend attributes garlic with many such tantalizing properties.

Second Prize Winner 1984 Recipe Contest: **Kathe Hewitt, La Jolla, CA**

1½ pounds Monterey Jack cheese

30 cloves fresh garlic

4 cups or more peanut oil

1 tablespoon Italian seasoning

3 eggs, beaten

2 cups all-purpose flour

3 cups French bread-crumbs*

3 tablespoons chopped fresh parsley

1 small jar marinara sauce

* Use day-old bread to prepare crumbs in a food processor. Dry packaged crumbs may be used but are not as attractive when fried.

Slice cheese into 30 slices about ¼-inch thick. Peel garlic and slice each clove lengthwise into 6 ovals. Heat oil in a deep, heavy saucepan over medium-low heat. Add garlic ovals and simmer 5 to 7 minutes, being careful not to burn or brown the cloves. Remove when garlic floats to surface and is light brown in color. Drain on paper towels. Reserve oil for the cheese. Mince the fried garlic and mix with Italian seasoning. Spread half the cheese slices evenly with garlic mixture. Press remaining cheese slices onto garlic-prepared cheese slices to make 15 bars. Dip flour-coated pieces into beaten eggs, then into breadcrumbs mixed with parsley, being sure to cover the sides. Reheat oil to medium-high and fry cheese in oil, a few pieces at a time, until lightly browned, about 2 minutes. Skim particles from the oil as they accumulate. Drain cheese on paper towels and keep warm until all are fried. Serve with toothpicks and your favorite commercial marinara sauce for dipping.

Makes about 30 pieces.

APPETIZER GARLIC PUFFS

The garlic filling used to make this appetizer can also be used to stuff cold, cooked artichokes and cold, blanched green peppers or as a topping for cold, sliced meats.

Finalist 1984 Recipe Contest: **Roxanne Chan, Albany, CA**

Puff Pastry

1 small head fresh garlic, separated into cloves

¹/₂ cup butter

1 cup all-purpose flour

¹/₄ teaspoon salt

4 eggs

Garlic Filling

1 small head fresh garlic, separated into cloves

2 cups whipped cream (about ¹/₂ pint)

1 cup grated Parmesan cheese

1 green onion, finely chopped

2 tablespoons *each* chopped pimento, black olives, and roasted almonds

Cover garlic cloves with boiling water. Let stand 5 minutes, then drain, peel, and mince. In a saucepan, melt butter in 1 cup boiling water. Add garlic, flour and salt all at once. Cook and stir until mixture forms a ball. Remove from heat, and cool slightly. Add eggs, one at a time, beating after each addition until mixture is smooth. Drop by teaspoonfuls onto a greased baking sheet. Bake in 400-degree F. oven for 10 minutes. Reduce heat to 325 degrees F. and continue to cook for 20 to 25 minutes, or until golden. Remove from oven and cut in half. Cool. Fill with Garlic Filling (see recipe below).

To make the garlic filling: Cover garlic cloves with boiling water. Cook until cloves are soft. Peel and mash. Stir mashed garlic into whipped cream along with remaining ingredients.

Makes about 20 appetizer puffs.

PEANUTS AND SLIVERS

This is one snack or party treat that will disappear faster than you can refill the bowl. Or they may be too tasty to share! A true taste sensation for the serious garlic-holic!

Finalist 1984 Recipe Contest: **Fernanda S. De Luna, Daly City, CA**

2 pounds peanuts, raw, shelled and skinned (about 6 cups)

6 whole heads fresh garlic, peeled and sliced to make about 2 ½ cups slivered garlic

Vegetable oil for frying peanuts and garlic separately

Salt to taste

Place peanuts in a wok preheated to medium-high with enough oil to cover peanuts. Stir peanuts constantly, being careful not to burn them. As peanuts begin to brown slightly, lower heat to simmer, and continue stirring until peanuts are light golden brown. Drain well in a wire basket and let cool. Place garlic in a skillet preheated with 1 ½ cups vegetable oil to medium-high. Stir garlic constantly to attain a consistent color and to prevent burning or sticking. As garlic browns slightly, reduce heat to low, and continue stirring. Cook until garlic is crisp and light golden brown. Drain garlic in the same manner as peanuts, breaking up any clusters. Cool. Combine peanuts and garlic and salt to taste. Store in airtight containers until ready to devour!

Makes about 6 cups.

TEXAS SURPRISE

A two-time finalist in the Contest, this creative cook devised a recipe guaranteed to delight garlic lovers everywhere. Whole cloves are cooked inside spicy meatballs that can be prepared ahead and frozen before baking. Keep on hand for a few drop-in friends or a crowd. If you freeze them, do not thaw, just add 5 to 10 minutes to the baking time.

Finalist 1982 Recipe Contest: **Karen Mahshi, Concord, CA**

50 to 60 cloves fresh garlic, peeled

12 ounces sharp Cheddar cheese

¹/₃ cup fresh parsley leaves, stems removed

1 to 3 jalapeño peppers (optional)

6 cloves fresh garlic

6 ounces hot pork sausage

6 ounces mild pork sausage

1¹/₄ cups buttermilk baking mix

Blanch 50 to 60 garlic cloves in boiling water 3 to 4 minutes. Drain and set aside to cool. In a food processor, shred the cheese. Remove and set aside. Allow cheese and sausage to come to room temperature. In a dry food processor bowl, chop parsley and peppers (if used). Crush 6 garlic cloves and add to processor, along with sausages and buttermilk mix. Process until well incorporated. Add cheese, and process only until well combined. Shape into 50 or 60 small balls, inserting one whole blanched garlic clove into each ball. At this point, balls may be frozen for baking at a later time. To bake at once, place balls on an ungreased baking sheet. Bake at 325 degrees F. for 20 to 25 minutes, or until golden brown. Serve hot as an appetizer or with a bowl of plain yogurt for dipping.

Makes 50 to 60 appetizers.

GARLIC FRITTERS

This is a variation on the French beignets so popular in New Orleans as well as in France. The garlic is included in the rich egg batter. The filling is made with sour cream flavored with Parmesan cheese and oregano. For more garlic flavor, try adding some fresh minced garlic to the filling as well.

Regional Winner 1984 Recipe Contest: **Helen Marty, Phoenix, AZ**

10 large cloves fresh garlic

¹/₄ teaspoon salt

6 tablespoons butter

1 cup water

1 cup flour

4 eggs

3 to 4 pounds fat for
   deep-frying

¹/₄ cup sour cream

¹/₄ cup grated Parmesan
   cheese

Dash powdered oregano

Finely chop the garlic, add salt and mash into a paste. Place butter, garlic and water in a saucepan and bring to a boil. Add flour, stirring quickly into a mass. Remove from heat. Add eggs, one at a time, incorporating thoroughly. Form the dough into small bite-sized mounds and deep-fry at about 370 degrees F. until golden brown. Drain on paper towels. Slice each fritter into two pieces. Combine sour cream, Parmesan and oregano and place ½ teaspoon of the mixture onto half of each fritter, and top with the other half.

Makes about 4 dozen fritters.

Onward garlic. This innocent herb
has staying power.

   —Kansas City Star

WHOLE GARLIC APPETIZER

An especially tart and tangy tidbit, this versatile snack or appetizer will keep in the refrigerator for up to ten days.

Finalist 1984 Recipe Contest: **Patrick Markey, Los Angeles, CA**

¹/₂ cup olive oil

8 whole heads fresh garlic

2 large sweet red onions, quartered

1 tablespoon whole peppercorns

4 stalks celery, chopped

4 medium carrots, sliced

¹/₄ teaspoon *each* fresh rosemary, thyme, oregano, marjoram, coriander, and basil

³/₄ cup white wine vinegar

¹/₄ cup dry white wine

¹/₂ cup water

8 to 10 bay leaves

¹/₂ teaspoon dry mustard

1 (4-ounce) can pickled green chiles

Heat oil in a skillet. Peel outer covering from garlic heads and take a ¹/₂- inch slice from the top of each head, exposing the meat of the cloves, but leaving the heads intact. Sauté garlic, onions, and peppercorns in oil for 3 minutes. Add celery, carrots, rosemary, thyme, oregano, marjoram, coriander, and basil. Sauté 5 minutes, stirring continuously. Add vinegar, wine, water, bay leaves and dry mustard. Simmer 10 minutes. Stir in chiles and simmer 3 minutes. Remove from heat, and strain, reserving garlic and 1 cup cooking liquid. Place garlic heads in a flat baking dish. Pour reserved liquid over the garlic, cover, and refrigerate. Serve cold as an appetizer for spreading on French bread or crackers. Also can be enjoyed as a relish, or cloves can be peeled and mixed into salads.

Makes 8 servings.

OYSTERS GILROY

The unusual anise-like flavor of the Pernod used in this recipe helps to create a sauce of intriguing complexity which blends very well with the oysters. An excellent first course for a very special dinner.

Finalist 1984 Recipe Contest: **Judge Steven E. Halpern, Emeryville, CA**

12 medium cloves fresh garlic, unpeeled

¹/₂ ripe avocado

³/₄ teaspoon salt

¹/₈ teaspoon black pepper

¹/₁₆ teaspoon cayenne pepper

3 tablespoons Pernod

2 tablespoons Worcestershire

2 tablespoons heavy cream

4 tablespoons melted butter

2 dozen medium-sized oysters in-the-half-shell

Rock salt

Wrap garlic in aluminum foil and bake in 325-degree F. oven for 30 minutes. Cool to room temperature. Pinch cloves and squeeze out garlic. Place in a food processor with remaining ingredients except butter and oysters, and process until mixture is thoroughly puréed. Then add butter in a slow stream until incorporated into the purée. Place oysters in-the-half-shell on a bed of rock salt in a baking pan. Bake at 450 degrees F. on the middle rack of the oven for 6 minutes. Remove. Cover each oyster with purée and return to the oven for 1 minute. Serve with sourdough bread and dry white wine.

Makes 4 to 6 appetizer servings.

TOASTED ALMOND CHEESE BALL

This rich and attractive appetizer is good and garlicky and all the better when aged a little.

Recipe Contest entry: **Nancy Brackmann, Pittsburgh, PA**

2 (8-ounce) packages cream
    cheese, softened

2 cups grated sharp cheese

3 cloves fresh garlic, minced

Dash Tabasco

1 cup slivered almonds

1 tablespoon butter

Combine the first four ingredients and form into a ball. In a skillet, toast the almonds in butter until browned. Cool and insert, one by one, into the cheese ball. Wrap in foil and allow to ripen in the refrigerator at least 48 hours. May then be frozen, if desired.

Makes a 2-pound cheese ball.

Baked and Stuffed Garlic Clams

This marvelous hors d'oeuvre is elegant and a snap to prepare. Serve with a dry California or Italian white wine, such as Sauvignon Blanc or Soave. Or serve champagne to heighten the festive mood.

Finalist 1984 Recipe Contest: **Rosina Wilson, Albany, CA**

20 to 30 cloves fresh garlic

3 (6 ½-ounce) cans chopped clams, drained (about 1 ½ cups) *or* the equivalent amount of steamed, chopped fresh clams

¾ cup butter, softened

1 tablespoon fresh oregano *or* 1 teaspoon dried

⅓ cup frozen or fresh cooked spinach

¼ cup sherry

1 cup French breadcrumbs

¼ cup minced parsley

2 tablespoons lemon juice

2 teaspoons pine nuts or chopped walnuts

½ teaspoon salt

¼ teaspoon *each* nutmeg, black pepper, and cayenne pepper

Sliced fresh garlic cloves dipped in olive oil, pine nuts, cayenne, and lemon wedges for garnish

Mince or press garlic to make ¾ cup. In a large bowl, combine garlic and other ingredients, except garnishes, and spoon generously into clam or scallop shells. Decorate each with a slice of garlic, pine nuts, and a sprinkle of cayenne pepper. Bake at 375 degrees F. for 25 to 30 minutes until breadcrumbs are golden brown and centers are cooked through. Serve piping hot with lemon wedges.

Makes about 6 servings.

WOWCHOS

This recipe for nachos with whole baked garlic cloves for extra flavor had the judges rolling their eyes with delight as they awarded second place to its creator.

Second Prize Winner 1983 Recipe Contest: **Leonard Brill, San Francisco, CA**

2 large heads fresh garlic, separated into cloves and peeled

2 tablespoons oil

Tortilla chips

¼ cup chopped red onion

1 (4-ounce) can chopped green chiles

⅓ cup sliced pimento-stuffed olives (optional)

1½ cups grated Pepper Jack cheese

Chopped cilantro

Chopped green onion tops

Coat garlic cloves with oil and bake in 375-degree F. oven for 30 minutes, or until soft and golden. Cover the bottom of a 9 x 12-inch metal baking pan with overlapping tortilla chips. Distribute garlic, onion, chiles, and olives over the chips. Cover with cheese and bake at 400 degrees F. for 5 minutes, or until cheese melts. Top with cilantro and green onion, and serve.

Makes about 4 appetizer servings.

STINKY CHEESE

Easy to make, this excellent cheese spread is great to have on hand for stuffing celery, spreading on crackers, for grilled cheese sandwiches, or as a topping for toasty French bread.

Recipe Contest entry: **Martin T. Quinlan, Woodland, CA**

2 pounds sharp Cheddar *or* Tillamook cheese

I pound Monterey Jack cheese

I (4-ounce) can whole green chiles

I (4-ounce) jar pimentos

10 to 14 cloves fresh garlic

½ cup dried minced onion

⅛ teaspoon ground pepper

Garlic powder

¾ cup mayonnaise

I cup water

Grate cheeses into a shallow pan or mixing bowl. Dice chile peppers and pimentos and sprinkle over grated cheese. Press garlic cloves, adding both juice and pulp to cheese. Generously sprinkle powdered garlic over all. Thoroughly mix together; then add mayonnaise and blend, adding water as needed to attain a smooth mixture. Store in airtight container at least two days before using.

Makes about 8 cups.

Oh, the miracle clove! Not only does garlic taste good, it cures baldness and tennis elbow, too.

—*Los Angeles Magazine*

PEOPLE-ALWAYS-ASK-FOR-THIS-RECIPE PARTY DIP

The best part of this recipe is when all the dip is gone and all that's left is the bread soaked in all those delicious ingredients. Just break up the bread and pass it around!

Finalist 1983 Recipe Contest: **Betty Shaw, Santee, CA**

1 loaf sheepherders bread

¼ pound butter

1 bunch green onions, chopped

12 cloves fresh garlic, minced finely

8 ounces cream cheese, at room temperature

16 ounces sour cream

12 ounces Cheddar cheese, grated

1 (10-ounce) can artichoke hearts (packed in water, not marinated), drained and cut into quarters

6 small French rolls, sliced thinly, but not all the way through

Cut a hole in the top of the bread loaf about 5 inches in diameter. Remove soft interior bread from the cut portion and discard. Reserve the crust to make "lid" for the loaf. Scoop out most of the soft interior bread to make a hollow loaf. In about 2 tablespoons butter, sauté green onions and half the garlic until onions wilt. Do not burn! Cut cream cheese into small chunks; add onions, garlic, sour cream, and Cheddar cheese. Mix well. Fold in artichoke hearts. Place mixture into the hollowed out loaf. Place the lid on the loaf and wrap in a double thickness of heavy-duty aluminum foil. Bake in a 350-degree F. oven 1½ to 2 hours. Spread remaining butter and garlic onto thinly sliced French bread. Wrap in foil and bake with the stuffed loaf for the last 30 minutes. When ready, remove foil and serve, using French bread slices to scoop out the dip.

Serves 10 to 12 as an appetizer.

AUNTIE PEGGY'S GARLIC SPREAD

Named for a favorite auntie, this creamy garlic spread is enough for two whole loaves of French bread. Great as a topping for potatoes, pasta, and veggies.

Recipe Contest entry: **Denise Domeniconi, San Francisco, CA**

6 cloves fresh garlic, peeled

6 green onions

I (8-ounce) package cream cheese, softened

2 cups shredded Cheddar cheese

2 tablespoons mayonnaise

3 teaspoons soy sauce

In a blender or food processor, mince garlic. Add onions and chop finely. Add cream cheese and mix thoroughly. Then add remaining ingredients and process until well blended. Spread onto halved loaves of French bread and place under the broiler until bubbly.

Makes about 3 cups.

MUSHROOMS OF THE AUVERGNE

The creator of this recipe recommends that you set the mood by playing "Songs of the Auvergne" while you put the finishing touches on this do-ahead starter course. The aroma of fresh garlic and the country songs of France are a perfect blend.

Recipe Contest entry: **Bob Comara, Los Angeles, CA**

12 medium mushrooms

3 to 4 tablespoons butter

10 leaves fresh spinach,
    washed and drained

3 large cloves fresh garlic,
    minced (about ½ teaspoon)

3 tablespoons grated
    Parmesan cheese

¼ teaspoon salt

¼ cup dry white wine

2 teaspoons water

Wipe mushrooms with a damp paper towel to remove surface dirt and remove stems. Place mushroom caps, tops down, in a well-buttered casserole dish. Blanch spinach in boiling water 3 minutes, rinse in cold water, and drain. Thoroughly combine garlic and butter. Mince spinach and blend with garlic butter. Fill mushroom caps evenly with butter mixture and sprinkle each with Parmesan cheese and salt. Cover with plastic wrap and refrigerate until ready to bake. When ready, heat oven to 300 degrees F., add wine and water to bottom of the casserole dish, and bake 20 minutes until mushrooms are cooked but still firm.

Makes 12 appetizers.

Mushrooms alla 'Rissa

Mushrooms stuffed with a combination of nutritious ingredients are a favorite of the Mayrons' three-year-old daughter who even likes them for breakfast!

Recipe courtesy of **Cindy Mayron, Gilroy, CA**

24 fresh mushrooms (about 1 pound)

1 medium onion, finely chopped

8 tablespoons butter or margarine

4 to 6 cloves garlic, chopped

2 tablespoons soy sauce

1 teaspoon sherry

Dash pepper

³/₄ cup Grape Nuts® cereal

8 ounces mozzarella cheese, shredded

Remove stems from mushrooms and chop fine. Wipe mushroom caps with damp paper towels and set aside. Sauté onion in 4 tablespoons butter over medium-high heat until crispy-brown, but not burned. Add 1 tablespoon butter, garlic, stems, 1 tablespoon soy sauce, sherry, and pepper. Cook until mushrooms are soft and have changed color. Add cereal and raise heat to high. Cook, stirring constantly, until moisture is absorbed. Add 1 to 2 tablespoons cereal, if needed. Remove from heat and let cool. Add cheese and mix thoroughly. Stuff mushroom caps with cooked mixture and place in 9 x 13-inch baking pan. Top each with remaining soy sauce and butter. Bake at 350 degrees F. for 15 minutes until mushrooms are cooked and cheese is melted.

Makes 24 appetizers.

Garlic is the king of seasonings.

—*Indianapolis Star*

GARLIC SQUARES

For truly devoted garlic fans, this oven-baked treat is better than brownies!

Recipe Contest entry: **Catherine A. Peters, San Francisco, CA**

1 cup fresh garlic, coarsely chopped

1 cup onions, thinly sliced

1/4 cup plus 2 tablespoons butter

2 cups flour

2 teaspoons baking powder

1 teaspoon salt

2 tablespoons finely chopped parsley

1 teaspoon dill

1 cup milk

1/2 cup sharp Cheddar cheese

Preheat oven to 450 degrees F. Gently sauté garlic and onions in 2 tablespoons butter about 10 minutes until tender, but not brown. Sift flour, baking powder and salt into a mixing bowl. Cut in 1/4 cup butter until mixture is crumbly like cornmeal. Add parsley, dill, and milk; stir just until evenly moist. Pour into a well-greased 8 x 8-inch pan. Spread garlic and onions on top, then cover with cheese. Bake 25 to 30 minutes. Cool slightly and cut into squares.

Serves 8 to 10 as an appetizer.

THE GREATEST GUACAMOLE OLE!

A few tips from the chef: If the avocados aren't quite ripe, chop them very fine and add a few teaspoonfuls of sour cream or mayonnaise to the recipe. Don't omit the cilantro, as its flavor is essential. For a fiery flavor, use jalapeños, but be sure to wear rubber gloves to protect your hands will preparing them. This recipe will keep in the refrigerator for several days, but it's best when served the same day.

Recipe Contest entry: **Catherine Miller, San Francisco, CA**

4 ripe avocados, peeled and seeded

3 cloves fresh garlic, minced

Juice of 1 lime

1 bunch fresh cilantro, chopped

5 scallions, chopped

5 peperoncini, chopped, *or* 1 to 2 jalapeño peppers, minced

$1/2$ teaspoon salt *or* to taste

$1/4$ teaspoon Tabasco *or* to taste

2 medium tomatoes, chopped

Mash avocados, lime juice, and garlic and combine with a fork. Stir in cilantro, scallions, peppers, and seasonings. Stir briskly until smooth, then gently stir in chopped tomatoes.

Serves 8 to 10 as a dip with chips.

GARLIC-SPINACH SNACKS

Anyone who loves garlic and spinach will really enjoy this recipe. Make it ahead and freeze it for later use.

Recipe Contest entry: **Candy Barnhart, Hollywood, CA**

2 (10-ounce) packages frozen chopped spinach

4 eggs

1 (10 3/4-ounce) can cream of mushroom soup

1 large onion, finely chopped

1/2 cup canned mushrooms, stems and pieces, drained

1/4 cup grated Parmesan cheese

1/4 cup Italian breadcrumbs

8 cloves fresh garlic, minced

1/4 teaspoon *each* ground oregano and dried basil

1/8 teaspoon coarsely ground black pepper

In a saucepan, heat spinach in just enough water to cover until completely thawed. Drain well. Beat eggs in a large mixing bowl. Add remaining ingredients and spinach and mix well. Turn into a greased 11 x 7 x 1½-inch glass baking dish and bake in a preheated 375-degree F. oven for 35 minutes, or until set to the touch. Serve slightly warm or cold, cut into 1½-inch squares.

Makes about 36 snacks.

ALL-AMERICAN EGG ROLLS

True to its immigrant origins, Chinese egg roll wrappers, Polish sausage, and French mustard combine with garlic for an all-American appetizer.

Recipe Contest entry: **Patricia Trinchero, Gilroy, CA**

I quart cooking oil

15 cloves fresh garlic, peeled

½ cup mayonnaise

½ cup softened cream cheese

2 heaping tablespoons
    prepared mustard

4 Polish sausages

I egg

¼ teaspoon milk

8 large egg roll wrappers

Chopped parsley

Heat oil in a frying pan to medium high, about 350 degrees F. Combine garlic, mayonnaise, cheese, and mustard in a blender until smooth. Remove from blender. Cut each sausage into two shorter halves and score lengthwise. Beat egg and milk with a fork until smooth. Place each sausage half at end of an egg roll wrapper, add a dollop of mustard sauce and roll up the sausage in the wrapper, sealing the ends with the egg mixture. Fry in hot oil until lightly browned on all sides. Garnish with chopped parsley and serve with extra mustard sauce.

Makes 8 servings.

The soul of pesto may be basil,
but its heart is garlic.

—*Pittsburgh Press*

PESTO MUSHROOMS

Large cheese-stuffed mushrooms are topped with tangy pesto sauce and baked for 15 minutes, just until all the flavors blend. If fresh basil isn't available, fresh spinach can be substituted.

Recipe Contest entry: **Jonny Butcher, North Highlands, CA**

16 large fresh mushrooms

2 or more ounces feta cheese

Pesto

2 1/2 cups lightly packed fresh basil leaves *or* 2 1/2 cups spinach leaves and 3 tablespoons dried basil

5 ounces Parmesan cheese, cut into chunks, *or* 1 cup grated Parmesan

3 cloves fresh garlic, peeled

1/4 cup shelled walnuts

1/3 cup extra virgin olive oil

Clean mushrooms and remove stems. Place mushroom caps, hollow-side up, on a rimmed 10 x 15-inch baking sheet. Fill each cap with feta cheese and set aside.

To make the pesto: In a food processor, combine basil, Parmesan cheese, garlic, and walnuts until thoroughly incorporated. With the processor running, slowly drizzle in oil and continue processing 5 to 10 seconds longer until well mixed. Top stuffed mushroom caps with about 1 tablespoon pesto and bake in a preheated oven at 375 degrees F. for 15 to 20 minutes.

Makes 5 to 6 servings.

DIP WITH ZIP

Whether you tone it down or spice it up, serve this zippy dip with fresh, fried tortilla chips for the best taste. Delicious with vegetables, too, or spread on a sandwich.

Recipe Contest entry: **Florence M. Zimmer, El Centro, CA**

I cup sour cream

I (3-ounce) package cream
cheese, softened

5 green onions, finely chopped

4 cloves fresh garlic, minced

3 tablespoons chopped chiles
or to taste

2 tablespoons salsa *or* to taste

2 jalapeño peppers, seeded and
chopped

Salt and pepper to taste

Stir all ingredients together, cover, and refrigerate until flavors have blended before serving.

Makes 1 1/2 cups.

MEXI-GILROY GARLIC DIP

House Rules: "No socializing or kissing allowed until everyone has tasted this garlicky dip." And it's great for discouraging party crashers. One friendly "Hi-i-i-i" is bound to send them scurrying.

Recipe Contest entry: **Sylvia Barber, Danville, CA**

I cup small curd cottage cheese

I cup real mayonnaise

I (4-ounce) can diced green chiles

I (4-ounce) can sliced black olives

6 cloves fresh garlic, minced

4 green onions, with tops, finely diced

I large tomato, finely chopped

Salt and pepper to taste

Combine all ingredients, cover, and refrigerate. Serve with chips or vegetables.

Makes 4 cups.

GARLIC HERB DIP

This creamy dip can be thinned with ⅔ cup milk or buttermilk to make a delicious salad dressing, or add 2 egg yolks and ¼ cup milk and pour over chicken before baking.

Recipe Contest entry: **Paula Linville, Aloha, OR**

I cup sour cream

½ cup mayonnaise

4 large cloves fresh garlic, minced

4 full sprigs fresh parsley, finely chopped

2 tablespoons Worcestershire sauce

I heaping tablespoon finely minced onion

I tablespoon dill weed

I teaspoon seasoned salt

3 drops Tabasco *or* to taste

Combine all ingredients thoroughly, cover, and refrigerate overnight or up to four days for more potent flavor. Serve with dippers of your choice.

Makes about 1½ cups.

FRESH GARLIC VEGETABLE DIP

Although there are vegetables in the dip itself, fresh vegetables for dipping also work well with this flavorful and healthful appetizer.

Recipe Contest entry: **Susan Centrone, Sepulveda, CA**

1 carrot, finely chopped

1/2 cup peeled and chopped cucumber

1/3 cup chopped zucchini

2 green onions, finely chopped

1 (8-ounce) package cream cheese, softened

1/2 cup sour cream

2 large cloves fresh garlic, minced

1/2 teaspoon salt

1/2 teaspoon dill weed

3 drops Tabasco

Combine all ingredients, cover, and refrigerate. Perfect served with wheat crackers.

Makes about 2 1/2 cups.

MANNY'S PORTUGUESE GARLIC DIP

Manny says this is soooo garlicky and soooo good that it always receives raves from friends and strangers alike.

Recipe Contest entry: **Manny Santos, Carmichael, CA**

1 (8-ounce) package cream
  cheese, softened

6 to 8 or more large cloves
  fresh garlic, minced

³/₄ to 1 cup mayonnaise

1 teaspoon Worcestershire
  sauce *or* to taste

Salt and pepper to taste

Combine all ingredients thoroughly, using just enough mayonnaise to reach preferred spreading or dipping consistency. Serve with chips for dipping or crackers for spreading.

Makes 2 cups.

GARLIC VEGGIE DIP

Water chestnuts are a succulent and surprising addition to this easy-to-prepare dip.

Recipe Contest entry: **Mrs. Milton Falk, Onaka, KS**

I cup sour cream

I cup mayonnaise

I teaspoon instant minced garlic

¼ cup chopped onion

¼ cup chopped parsley

¼ cup chopped water chestnuts

Combine all ingredients, cover, and chill. Serve with crisp vegetables.

Makes 2½ cups.

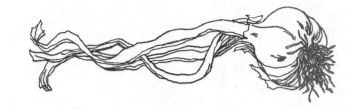

Garlic Artichoke Dip

Fresh garlic combines with artichokes from nearby Castroville to produce a tasty dip which is equally good with crispy chips or fresh vegetables. And it couldn't be easier!

Recipe courtesy of **Barbara Hay, Gilroy, CA**

3 cloves fresh garlic, peeled

2 (8 ½-ounce) cans artichoke hearts, drained

I cup grated Parmesan cheese

I cup mayonnaise

Juice of I lemon

Dash Tabasco

Fresh vegetables *or* chips for dipping

In a food processor, chop garlic and artichoke hearts until medium fine. Place in a small baking dish, add remaining ingredients, and mix thoroughly. Bake in 350-degree F. oven for 30 minutes, or until golden brown on top. Serve with vegetables or chips for dipping.

Makes about 6 servings.

CREAMY GARLIC GUACAMOLE

Don't relegate this garlic lovers' guacamole to the chip-and-dip department. Use it as a topping for poultry dishes, dolloped into soups, or spread on pita or other breads before adding meat or cheese to make ultra-savory sandwiches.

Recipe Contest entry: **Becky Ayres, Salem, OR**

1 large *or* 2 small heads fresh
    garlic

1 ripe avocado

1 (3-ounce) package cream
    cheese, softened

3 tablespoons sour cream

1 tablespoon fresh lemon juice

1/4 teaspoon salt

Place whole head(s) of garlic in a baking dish, drizzle with oil, and roast in 350-degree F. oven for about 1 hour, or until garlic is soft. When cool, gently separate cloves and squeeze out garlic into a blender or bowl. Peel and pit avocado, and add to garlic, along with remaining ingredients. Blend or mash until smooth. Serve with vegetables and chips or as a topping for Mexican dishes.

Makes approximately 1 1/2 cups.

DRAGON DIP

This garlic-cheese dip should be served warm in a chafing dish with chips, crackers or, better yet, with fresh vegetables.

Recipe Contest entry: **Cynthia Kannenberg, Brown Deer, WI**

1 (8-ounce) package cream cheese

6 cloves fresh garlic, finely minced *or* 1 1/2 teaspoons garlic powder

2 cups grated Cheddar cheese

6 tablespoons half-and-half

1 teaspoon Worcestershire sauce

1/2 teaspoon dry mustard

1/4 teaspoon onion salt

3 drops Tabasco

6 slices bacon, fried crisp and crumbled

Combine all ingredients, except bacon, in a double boiler. Cook, stirring continuously, until smooth and blended. Add bacon and heat through. Place in a chafing dish and serve with dippers of your choice.

Makes 3 cups.

DAVID'S PRESERVED PEPPERS

Preserved peppers make a great addition to appetizers, salads, antipasto plates, or just for nibbling. Green bell peppers can be used if red peppers are not available, but the color is not as attractive.

Recipe Contest entry: **David Martin, Gilroy, CA**

4 quarts water

6 tablespoons salt

2 cups white distilled vinegar

7 to 9 pounds red bell peppers

25 whole black peppercorns

15 cloves fresh garlic, peeled and halved

5 sprigs fresh dill

5 bay leaves

In a large pot, boil water with salt, until dissolved. Remove from heat and add vinegar. Cut peppers in half lengthwise, remove seeds, and cut into ½-inch thick strips. Into five 1-quart canning jars, place 5 whole peppercorns, 6 halves of garlic, a sprig of dill, and 1 bay leaf. Fill jars with pepper strips, and pour brine over to about ¼ inch from the top of each jar. Scald lid under boiling water and seal as manufacturer directs. Place sealed jars in a deep pot with a rack and add boiling water to cover. Do not pour water directly onto the jars as they may crack. Cover pot, heat water to boiling, and boil gently about 10 minutes, reducing heat if necessary. Remove jars from water bath and place upright on newspapers to cool. Store in a cool place at least 2 weeks prior to serving. Best served chilled.

Makes 5 quarts.

Garlic Popcorn Balls

Devilishly delicious, these are a great snack to accompany beer and football.

Recipe Contest entry: **Linda Tarvin, Morgan Hill, CA**

50 cloves (about 4 heads)
 fresh garlic

2 teaspoons salt

4 cups (about 1 pound)
 shredded Cheddar cheese

5 quarts popped corn (about
 ¹/₂ cup unpopped corn)

Peel garlic and mince with salt to prevent sticking and to absorb garlic juices. Toss garlic with cheese. In a large glass or plastic bowl, make alternate layers of popped corn and garlic-cheese mixture, coating popcorn as evenly as possible, especially at edge of the bowl. Place in a microwave oven and cook 1 minute. Shake the bowl gently; rotate 180 degrees and cook 1 more minute. Do not overcook. Immediately turn out onto a cookie sheet and quickly shape into plum-sized balls. Place balls on sheets of waxed paper.

Makes 4 dozen popcorn balls.

Vegetables, Sides, and Savory Pies

ONIONS STUFFED WITH GARLIC AND CHESTNUTS

Onions and garlic are "kissin' cousins" in the plant kingdom with quite different individual flavors which blend together beautifully in this elegant baked vegetable dish.

Regional Winner 1984 Recipe Contest: **Dr. Joyce M. Johnson, Atlanta, GA**

4 large Spanish onions

4 slices bacon, chopped

1 tablespoon butter

1 whole head fresh garlic, peeled and chopped

1 (8-ounce) can water chestnuts, drained and chopped

¼ cup breadcrumbs

½ teaspoon salt

¼ teaspoon black pepper

1 cup apple cider

Place the unskinned onions in boiling water for about 5 minutes. Remove and cool. Cut off tops and peel. Scoop out the insides and chop. Set aside. In a frying pan, cook bacon until crisp. Drain off fat, add butter and sauté the bacon bits, chopped onion, and the chopped cloves of garlic until just lightly brown. Add the water chestnuts and breadcrumbs and continue to brown another 3 minutes. Add salt and pepper. Fill each onion with the mixture. Place in a casserole. Pour apple cider over the stuffed onions and bake at 375 degrees F. for 45 to 50 minutes.

Makes 4 servings.

EGGPLANT DELIGHT

Developed in 1900 by Elizabeth Powell's grandmother, Elizabeth Shallow Bowden, this exceptional dish has been updated somewhat over the years. It qualifies as a vegetarian dinner and can be doubled to feed a large crowd.

Recipe Contest entry: **Elizabeth Powell, Media, PA**

4 eggplants

4 cloves fresh garlic, peeled

¹/₂ pound *each* shredded Cheddar and Swiss cheese

3 to 4 tablespoons butter

Lightly coat two 12 x 9 x 2-inch ovenproof casseroles with nonstick spray. Peel and slice eggplant lengthwise about ¼-inch thick. Slice garlic lengthwise in paper-thin slices. Arrange layers of eggplant and garlic in casseroles with cheeses and dots of butter separating each, ending with a top layer of garlic and butter. Bake at 375 degrees F. about 45 minutes, or until deeply brown in color, bubbly and crusted.

Makes 10 ample servings.

GARLIC EGGPLANT

An Asian fusion-style dish that combines flavors from Thailand and China.

Regional Winner 1982 Recipe Contest: **Ilene Hellman, Kennett, MO**

^{1}/$_2$ pound ground pork

2 tablespoons soy sauce

1 ^{1}/$_2$ pounds eggplant, peeled and cut into ^{1}/$_2$-inch squares

1 large onion, chopped

^{1}/$_3$ cup sherry

5 tablespoons oyster sauce

2 teaspoons sesame oil

1 teaspoon sugar

3 tablespoons peanut oil

10 cloves fresh garlic, minced

1 tablespoon chili paste with garlic

^{1}/$_2$ teaspoon ginger, minced

In a small bowl, add 1 tablespoon soy sauce to pork, and set aside. Combine eggplant and onion in another bowl. Mix sherry, oyster sauce, remaining soy sauce, sesame oil, and sugar in a third bowl, and set aside. Preheat a wok or electric skillet; add peanut oil, then add minced garlic, chili paste, and ginger. Cook for a few seconds, stirring constantly. Add pork mixture and stir-fry, stirring constantly, until pork loses its pink color. Add eggplant and onion mixture. Stir in sauce, adding more sherry as necessary for the liquid to cover about half the mixture in the wok. Cover, and cook on high heat about 7 minutes. If the sauce starts to evaporate before the eggplant is tender, add more sherry as needed. When eggplant is tender, uncover, and cook until most of the remaining sauce has evaporated. Serve immediately.

Makes 4 servings.

Artichokes alla Rosina

This winning recipe from a very talented lady combines steamed artichokes and whole cloves of garlic dipped in a tantalizing basil-laced aioli sauce, then drawn between the teeth to extract the pulp and sauce simultaneously. Thoroughly delightful! The name for the sauce, "Baioli," came from her daughter. It's a contraction of basil and aioli. Substitute fresh tarragon for "Taioli," fresh dill for "Daioli," or parsley for "Paioli."

Winner 1982 Recipe Contest: **Rosina Wilson, Albany, CA**

6 medium artichokes

6 large heads fresh garlic

I large lemon, halved

$^1/_2$ teaspoon salt

$^1/_2$ cup olive oil

Baioli Sauce

4 to 6 cloves fresh garlic, peeled

2 egg yolks

3 tablespoons lemon juice

I tablespoon Dijon-style mustard

$^1/_2$ teaspoon salt

I cup olive oil

$^1/_2$ cup fresh basil leaves

Clean artichokes and place in a large kettle. Peel off papery outer skin from garlic, leaving heads intact. Nestle garlic heads among artichokes. Add water to cover artichokes half way, squeeze in juice from lemons, and tuck in the lemon peels. Add salt and olive oil. Bring to a boil, and simmer 45 to 60 minutes, until tender, depending on size of the artichokes. Drain well. Serve warm or cold, with "Baioli" sauce. The garlic heads will be soft enough to eat like the artichokes, picking off cloves, pulling out pulp between the teeth, and discarding the skin.

To make the sauce: In a blender jar, place 4 to 6 cloves fresh garlic, peeled, 2 egg yolks, 3 tablespoons lemon juice, 1 tablespoon mustard, and $^1/_2$ teaspoon salt. Cover and blend until smooth. With the blender running, remove the cover, and very slowly pour in 1 cup of olive oil in a very thin stream. Replace cover, turn off the blender. Uncover, and scrape down sides. Adjust seasoning. Add $^1/_2$ cup fresh sweet basil leaves, and blend briefly, until coarsely chopped.

Makes 6 servings.

ARTICHOKE PIE

Serve this dish warm or cold, as an hors d'oeuvre, or as a main dish lunch. It's delicious no matter how you serve it.

Regional Winner 1981 Recipe Contest: **Mrs. Lawrence d'Amico, Hackensack, NJ**

4 to 5 cloves fresh garlic

1 medium onion

2 tablespoons butter

3 large eggs

1 cup whipping cream

1/2 cup shredded mozzarella cheese

1/4 cup grated Parmesan cheese

Salt and pepper to taste

1 (8 1/2-ounce) can artichoke hearts*

1 unbaked 9-inch pastry shell**

* Or use 1 small package frozen artichoke hearts. Parboil and drain well.

** Use your favorite recipe, or a frozen, deep, 9-inch shell.

Mince garlic and thinly slice onion. Sauté in butter until soft and golden; do not brown. Beat eggs and add cream, cheeses, salt and pepper to taste, and garlic-onion mixture. Drain and cut artichokes in quarters. Add to egg mixture and gently poor into pastry shell. Bake in the oven preheated 400 degrees F. about 45 minutes until set. Serve warm or cold as an entrée or appetizer.

Makes one 9-inch pie.

TOMATOES WILLIAM

Fresh whole tomatoes are scooped out and filled with a savory mixture of onion, sausage, garlic, and breadcrumbs, then baked with their caps on until juicy and tender.

Finalist 1982 Recipe Contest: **Bill Scales, Gilroy, CA**

6 medium to large tomatoes

Salt

Garlic powder

2 pounds ground sausage meat

2 tablespoons butter

3 onions, diced

4 cloves fresh garlic, minced

⅓ bunch fresh parsley, finely chopped

¼ cup breadcrumbs

Remove tops from tomatoes and set aside. Scoop out insides of tomatoes to make shells. Sprinkle tomato shells with salt and garlic powder and turn upside down on paper towels to drain. Brown the sausage in a buttered skillet. Drain and discard fat. Sauté onions and garlic in butter until soft. Combine with sausage, parsley, and breadcrumbs. Cook gently over medium heat for 5 minutes. Spoon into tomato shells and cover with reserved tomato tops. Sprinkle lightly with additional breadcrumbs. Bake, uncovered, at 325 degrees F. for 45 minutes.

Makes 6 servings.

Nothing beats the versatility of garlic, the great international seasoning.

—Los Angeles Times

BEST BROCCOLI

Prepare this dish well ahead of time so the broccoli can chill long enough to allow the flavors to permeate the dish. Then serve cold, preferably with a homemade garlic mayonnaise.

Recipe Contest entry: **Sara Janene Evans, San Luis Obispo, CA**

1 ½ pounds fresh broccoli

10 large cloves fresh garlic, unpeeled

⅓ cup red wine vinegar

3 tablespoons olive oil

2 teaspoons salt

Separate broccoli into flowerets with small stems, then peel main trunk and slice into strips. Crush garlic partially, using the flat side of a knife. Fill a large pot with water, add all ingredients, being sure that broccoli stems are submerged, and cook, covered, until tender. Drain and refrigerate several hours or overnight.

Makes 4 servings.

GARLIC POTATOES WITH CHEESE SAUCE

Bread may be the staff of life, but potatoes run a close second. You can never have too many good recipes for serving potatoes. This regional contest winner kept her's simple, but it is simply delicious.

Regional Winner 1981 Recipe Contest: **Harriett Macht, Santa Rosa, CA**

Potatoes

3 large potatoes

1 medium onion

6 or more large cloves fresh garlic

2 tablespoons butter

½ cup grated Cheddar cheese

Cheese Sauce

2 tablespoons butter

2 tablespoons flour

½ teaspoon *each* salt and dry mustard

Dash of paprika

¾ cup grated Cheddar cheese

½ cup milk

Pare and thinly slice potatoes; peel and mince onion; peel garlic. Grease a 10-inch baking dish or casserole. Cover bottom with one layer of potatoes. Sprinkle with minced onion. Using a garlic press, press 2 cloves garlic and sprinkle over potatoes. Dot potatoes with a portion of the butter. Repeat until all potatoes are used, making 3 to 4 layers. Pour Cheese Sauce (see recipe below) over potatoes. Sprinkle ½ cup grated cheese on top. Cover and bake in a moderate 350-degree F. oven for 30 minutes. Uncover, and bake 30 minutes longer until potatoes are tender.

To make the cheese sauce: Melt butter in a saucepan. Blend in flour. Slowly stir in milk. Cook over moderate heat, stirring continuously, until sauce is smooth and slightly thickened. Blend in salt and dry mustard, a generous dash of paprika, and ¾ cup grated Cheddar cheese. Heat, stirring, until cheese melts.

Makes 6 generous servings.

GARLIC-CHEESE FILLED CARROTS

Rarely does anyone do anything quite so special with carrots. Prepare them ahead, if you wish, and bake about 20 minutes before serving. The sweetness of the cooked carrot and garlic makes a very happy blend.

Regional Winner 1982 Recipe Contest: **Jimmy Hobbs, Palacios, TX**

6 to 8 large carrots
 (about 1 pound)

1 teaspoon salt

¹/₂ teaspoon sugar

3 cloves fresh garlic

1¹/₂ cups grated mild Cheddar
 cheese

1 tablespoon milk

1 teaspoon finely chopped
 onion

¹/₈ teaspoon black pepper

Scrub carrots and scrape lightly. Cut into halves crosswise. Barely cover with boiling water, add ¹/₂ teaspoon salt and sugar, cover, and cook slowly until tender, 10 to 20 minutes, depending on size of carrots. Do not overcook. Drain and cool slightly. Simmer garlic in small amount of boiling water 1 minute. Drain, peel, and chop or mash to a pulp. Split each carrot half lengthwise down the center. Gently lift out core and mash to fine pulp, or process 3 to 4 seconds in a food processor. Add ¹/₂ cup of the cheese, mashed garlic, milk, onion, remaining ¹/₂ teaspoon salt, and pepper, and continue mashing or processing to a paste. Mound the mixture into half the carrot pieces and press the corresponding half over the filled portion. Place close together in a buttered 8-inch square pan or a decorative shallow casserole. Sprinkle the remaining cheese over all. Bake at 400 degrees F. for 10 to 15 minutes, until tops are lightly toasted.

Makes 4 servings.

VERY GARLIC ARTICHOKES

Artichokes are wonderful with just a little fresh garlic for seasoning, but this recipe includes oregano and sherry for an intriguing flavor boost. When prepared this way, there's nary a leaf left, claims Ms. Van Dam.

Recipe Contest entry: **Caroline Van Dam, Tarzana, CA**

4 medium to large artichokes

I head fresh garlic

¼ pound butter

½ to ¾ cup dry sherry

I teaspoon oregano

Steam or boil artichokes until tender; drain and arrange in serving dish, opening leaves slightly. Peel garlic and chop coarsely, or cut in thin slices. Sauté lightly in butter, add wine and oregano, and bring to a boil. Spoon sauce over artichokes, drizzling down through the leaves. Serve hot or cold as an appetizer or a vegetable course.

Makes 4 servings.

GARLIC GREEN BEANS

This spicy side dish would be appropriate served with any grilled or roasted meat or fish.

Recipe Contest entry: **Kathy Borges, Morgan Hill, CA**

2 pounds fresh green beans

¹/₄ pound bacon, diced

1 small onion, chopped

3 cloves fresh garlic, minced

¹/₂ green bell pepper, seeded and chopped

1 (8-ounce) can tomato sauce

³/₄ teaspoon Italian seasoning

¹/₂ teaspoon salt

¹/₄ teaspoon pepper

Wash beans, trim, and cut into 2-inch pieces. Steam until crisp-tender, approximately 7 to 10 minutes. Set aside. Meanwhile, in a large saucepan, fry bacon until crisp. Remove from pan with slotted spoon and set aside. Discard all but 3 tablespoons of bacon drippings. Add onion, garlic, and green pepper and cook over medium heat until soft, about 5 minutes. Add tomato sauce, seasonings, and reserved bacon. Simmer together for about 10 minutes to blend flavors. Add cooked beans and heat through.

Makes 6 to 8 servings.

Cooking with garlic works magic
with fresh vegetables.

—*Nashville Banner*

GREEN BEANS AU GARLIC

Served as an antipasto, these aromatic garlicky beans will get your taste buds working overtime.

Recipe Contest entry: **John Proynoff, Phoenix, AZ**

2 ½ pounds young fresh green
    beans

1 large onion, chopped

½ cup olive oil

1 teaspoon paprika

2 tomatoes, chopped

1 head garlic, peeled and
    crushed

2 tablespoons chopped parsley

1 teaspoon salt

Wash beans, trim, and cut in half. if very long. Cook, uncovered, in boiling water, or steam, about 15 minutes, until crisp-tender. Do not overcook. Drain and set aside. Meanwhile, in separate pan, sauté onion in oil until soft, add paprika, and cook 1 minute more before adding tomatoes, garlic, parsley, and salt. Simmer on low 8 to 10 minutes, stirring occasionally. Add beans and combine well. Refrigerate until ready to serve.

Makes 8 servings.

ITALIAN BROCCOLI

This is an old family recipe that has been enjoyed by the Kovatches for many generations. It's an excellent dish for entertaining as it can be made ahead of time and heated just before serving. Try it with cauliflower or cabbage.

Recipe Contest entry: **Mrs. A. Kovatch, Sr., River Ridge, LA**

1 large bunch broccoli

1 small onion, chopped

8 cloves fresh garlic, peeled and chopped

1/2 cup olive oil

1 cup Italian breadcrumbs

3/4 cup grated Parmesan cheese

1 egg, beaten slightly

Salt, pepper, and garlic powder to taste

Steam or boil broccoli until tender. Drain and coarsely mash. In a large skillet, sauté onion and garlic in oil. When onion begins to brown, add broccoli and stir to mix. Add breadcrumbs and cheese, and stir until well blended. Remove from heat and add egg. Stir again to blend; add seasonings, and stir. Place in a casserole and, when ready to serve, warm in 350-degree F. oven about 15 minutes.

Makes 6 servings.

CHEESY SPINACH

Easy, economical, and very good. Spinach not your favorite? Substitute other leafy greens such as chard or kale.

Recipe Contest entry: **Patricia Lentz, Sunland, CA**

I large bunch spinach *or* other leafy greens

2 onions, peeled and chopped

3 cloves fresh garlic, peeled and chopped *or* $1/2$ teaspoon powdered garlic

I cup cooked brown rice

$1/3$ cup or more grated cheese

2 tablespoons soy sauce

Thoroughly clean spinach, remove stems, and chop leaves and stems separately. In a wok or skillet, sauté stems, onion, and garlic until onions are translucent. Stir in cooked rice, incorporating well. Place spinach leaves on top of rice mixture. Cover pan and cook until spinach is wilted. Stir wilted spinach into the rice mixture. Add the cheese and season to taste with soy sauce. Stir until the cheese melts and holds the mixture together.

Makes about 3 servings.

BIG DADDY'S BIG-ON-FLAVOR SPINACH TREATS

We'd love to know whether Big Daddy developed this recipe, or just enjoyed it so much it was named in his honor.

Recipe Contest entry: **Thomas O. Davis, Waynesboro, MS**

2 (10-ounce) packages frozen chopped spinach, cooked and drained

10 cloves fresh garlic, finely chopped

3 cups commercial herb stuffing mix

6 eggs

$1/2$ cup melted butter

$1/2$ cup grated Parmesan-Romano cheese mixture

$1 1/4$ teaspoon salt

$1/4$ teaspoon Tabasco

1 ($10 3/4$-ounce) can condensed cream of celery soup

Combine all ingredients except soup. Shape into small balls. Place on a large, ungreased baking pan. Bake, uncovered, at 325 degrees F. for 20 to 25 minutes. Remove to serving dish. Heat soup to boiling and pour over treats. Serve hot.

Makes 8 to 10 servings.

MEDITERRANEAN RAINBOW

This dish is best served lukewarm with buttered French bread to sop up the sauce. It can be a light lunch, an antipasto, or a vegetable accompaniment to a simple (but garlicky) meat or chicken main course. Slightly chilled Beaujolais or fruity Zinfandel completes the meal.

Recipe Contest entry: **Rosina Wilson, Albany, CA**

1 cup peeled garlic cloves (2 to 4 heads)

¹/₂ pound *each* green and yellow zucchini

2 red and 2 green bell peppers

1 bunch baby carrots

¹/₂ cup olive oil

5 small hot chile peppers

1 large onion, thinly sliced

12 wrinkled black olives

4 anchovies, mashed

2 tablespoons lemon peel, cut into strips

Salt and pepper to taste

¹/₂ cup chopped parsley

Freshly grated Parmesan cheese

Cut garlic in slivers. Slice zucchini and bell peppers into long, thin julienne strips. Cut larger carrots into quarters or leave whole if very small. In a skillet, sauté garlic in oil slowly, along with chile peppers, about 5 minutes. Add onion and bell peppers, and sauté 5 minutes more. Add zucchini and carrots, stirring gently to coat with oil. Cover, and steam 5 minutes, then remove cover, add anchovies, olives, and lemon peel. Continue stirring until vegetables are cooked but still crunchy. Add salt and pepper; stir in parsley, and transfer all to serving platter. Top with Parmesan cheese.

Makes 6 servings.

NINA'S RATATOUILLE

A delicious, healthful, and satisfying dish. Try using this mixture to fill crepes and serve as a main dish. If rocambole (a relative of both garlic and shallots) is not available, increase the amount of garlic used.

Recipe Contest entry: **Nina Landy, Pacific Palisades, CA**

I medium eggplant, peeled and diced

2 to 3 tablespoons sesame oil

2 onions, peeled and sliced

3 shallots, peeled and sliced

3 cloves fresh garlic, minced

3 rocambole, squeezed in garlic press

2 zucchini, sliced

2 medium ripe tomatoes *or* I (16-ounce) can drained stewed tomatoes

I green bell pepper, sliced

I (8-ounce) can tomato sauce

¹/₂ cup dry white wine (optional)

¹/₂ teaspoon *each* dried basil and thyme

I bay leaf

Salt, pepper, and garlic powder to taste

Chopped fresh parsley

Freshly grated Parmesan cheese

Salt eggplant lightly, and let stand 15 minutes. Dry on paper towels. Heat oil in a skillet and sauté onions, shallots, garlic, and rocambole for 3 minutes until all are soft and onion is transparent. Add eggplant and zucchini and sauté 5 minutes until both are soft and lightly browned. Add all remaining ingredients except parsley and cheese. Cover, and continue cooking about 20 minutes until all vegetables are soft and tender. Garnish with parsley and sprinkle with cheese.

Makes 4 servings.

GARLIC JALAPEÑO POTATOES

Great for a potluck! The jalapeño cheese adds zesty flavor to au gratin potatoes.

Recipe Contest entry: **Mrs. Milton E. Falk, Onaga, MS**

8 medium red potatoes,
   cooked until tender

I green bell pepper, slivered

I (4-ounce) jar pimentos,
   drained

Salt and pepper to taste

¼ pound butter

2 tablespoons flour

3 cloves fresh garlic, minced

2 cups milk

2 cups jalapeño cheese, cubed

I½ cups crushed Rice Chex®
   cereal

Peel and slice potatoes. Layer in a buttered casserole with bell pepper and pimentos. Salt and pepper each layer to taste. Melt butter in a saucepan, add flour and minced garlic, and stir until well blended. Gradually add milk, stirring constantly. Add cheese. Stir until cheese melts. Pour over potatoes and top with crushed cereal. Bake 45 minutes at 350 degrees F.

Makes 8 to 10 servings.

ROASTED GARLIC POTATOES

A classic and very simple dish with only a few ingredients but lots of good flavor.

Recipe Contest entry: **Angela Rainero, Oakland, CA**

4 large baking potatoes, peeled

4 cloves fresh garlic

6 tablespoons butter

³/₄ cup grated Parmesan cheese

Salt and pepper

Cut potatoes in half lengthwise, then slice medium-thin and place in a large bowl. Mince or press garlic. Melt butter in a small saucepan and add garlic. Cook on medium heat for 1 minute. Add to potatoes with half the cheese and salt and pepper. Stir until potatoes are well coated. Pour into a greased shallow baking dish. Top with remaining cheese and bake at 400 degrees F., uncovered, until golden brown, about 30 minutes. Do not stir or turn during cooking.

Makes 6 servings.

SWEET AND SOUR GARLIC VEGETABLES

So easy and the flavors just keep unfolding.

Recipe Contest entry: **Nancy Stamatis, Union City, CA**

2 pounds fresh, sliced
    vegetables (carrots,
    broccoli, mushrooms,
    cauliflower, etc.)

4 tablespoons white wine
    vinegar

4 tablespoons sugar

1 1/2 teaspoons salt

4 tablespoons vegetable oil

4 cloves fresh garlic, peeled
    and sliced

Pare, trim, and slice vegetables. Combine vinegar, sugar, and salt in large jar. Add vegetables and shake to mix well. Cover and refrigerate overnight, shaking occasionally. In another smaller jar, mix oil and garlic (no need to refrigerate). At serving time, drain vegetables and place on a serving platter. Pour garlic oil over and serve with toothpicks.

Makes about 4 cups.

TRANSYLVANIAN CARROTS

Even vampires find this dish hard to resist!

Recipe Contest entry: **Tracy King, Glendale, CA**

1 pound carrots
6 to 8 cloves fresh garlic
4 or more tablespoons butter
½ teaspoon pepper
Salt and pepper to taste
Chopped fresh parsley

Peel carrots and slice diagonally into 1-inch lengths. Peel garlic and slice thinly lengthwise. Place carrots and garlic in 1½-quart saucepan with enough water to barely cover. Add butter and pepper and cook, covered, over medium heat until carrots are tender. Remove cover and cook over high heat until water has boiled away and carrots are glazed with butter, about 5 minutes. Salt to taste and garnish with chopped parsley.

Makes 4 servings.

ZIPPY ZUCCHINI FRITTERS

A delicious way to use the ever-abundant zucchini.

Recipe Contest entry: **Nancy Bruce, Fair Oaks, CA**

2 1/2 cups shredded zucchini

4 eggs

1 (4-ounce) can diced green
    chiles

3/4 cup dry breadcrumbs

1/3 cup grated Parmesan
    cheese

4 cloves fresh garlic, minced

1 teaspoon chicken flavored
    soup base

1/4 teaspoon pepper

Oil for frying

Grated Parmesan cheese
    for garnish

Squeeze as much water as possible from grated zucchini (leaves about 1 cup). Place all ingredients, except oil, in a bowl and mix well. Pour oil in a skillet to 1/8-inch depth and heat over medium heat. Drop batter into hot oil, 1 heaping tablespoon at a time, to make 8 fritters. Fry about 5 minutes on one side, turn, and fry until golden brown on the other side. Sprinkle lightly with additional Parmesan cheese, if desired. Serve immediately.

Makes 4 servings.

HEAVEN SCENT

Uncomplicated, but uncommonly good. Zucchini, mushrooms, and garlic make an unbeatable combination.

Recipe Contest entry: **Janice Smith, Delano, CA**

2 tablespoons butter

1 tablespoon olive oil

4 cloves fresh garlic, sliced

1 cup sliced fresh mushrooms

4 or 5 zucchini, sliced thin

1 teaspoon minced parsley

½ teaspoon thyme

Salt and pepper to taste

In a large skillet or wok, melt butter over high heat. Add olive oil and garlic, and stir for 1 minute. Add mushrooms and stir-fry for 3 minutes. Add zucchini and stir-fry 4 minutes more. Sprinkle in parsley, thyme, salt, and pepper. Stir, and serve immediately.

Makes 4 or 5 servings.

MYRNA'S STUFFED ZUCCHINI

The unusual stuffing calls for white beans, garbanzo beans, and, of course, garlic. If you cook the beans yourself, be sure to add a bay leaf to the water.

Recipe Contest entry: **Myrna Slade, San Francisco, CA**

6 medium zucchini

I bay leaf

6 cloves fresh garlic

1/2 cup chopped onion

1/4 cup chopped parsley

2 tablespoons butter

I large tomato, chopped

1/2 teaspoon *each* thyme, cumin, and oregano

Dash cayenne

Salt and pepper to taste

2 cups cooked white beans, drained

I cup cooked garbanzo beans, drained

2 tablespoons olive oil

Slice zucchini in half lengthwise; simmer in 1/2 inch of water with the bay leaf until tender, about 5 minutes. Cool slightly, and scoop out insides, leaving twelve 1/2-inch thick zucchini shells. Chop insides. Coarsely chop 4 cloves of garlic, and sauté with onion and parsley in butter until golden and soft, about 5 minutes. Stir in tomato and cook 1 minute more. Season with thyme, cumin, oregano, cayenne, salt, and pepper. Add chopped zucchini. Mash beans until semi-smooth and stir into vegetable mixture. Stuff into zucchini shells and place in a buttered baking dish. Mince remaining 2 cloves of garlic and mix with breadcrumbs and olive oil; sprinkle evenly over stuffed zucchini. Bake at 350 degrees F. for 10 to 15 minutes, until crumbs are golden and crisp and all is heated through.

Makes 6 servings.

ZUCCHINI ZAPI

Another delicious approach to preparing the prolific squash, serve this dish as a light lunch or on the side with grilled meats.

Recipe Contest entry: **Cynthia Kannenberg, Brown Deer, WI**

3 pounds fresh zucchini, sliced

½ cup chopped onion

6 tablespoons butter, softened

3 cloves fresh garlic, minced

10 saltine crackers, crushed

1 cup grated sharp Cheddar cheese

2 eggs, beaten

Seasoned salt and freshly ground pepper to taste

Italian seasoned dry breadcrumbs

Paprika and fresh parsley sprigs for garnish

Boil zucchini for 20 minutes. Drain and mash. Sauté onion in 2 tablespoons of butter and add to zucchini with garlic, crackers, cheese, remaining 4 tablespoons butter, eggs, and seasonings. Mix well. Pour into a greased 9 x 13-inch casserole and sprinkle with breadcrumbs. Bake at 350 degrees F. for 30 minutes. Garnish with paprika and sprigs of parsley.

Makes 6 servings.

ZUCCHINI LEAVES

Attractive presentation in addition to excellent flavor are two good reasons to prepare this stuffed zucchini recipe.

Recipe Contest entry: **Rose Montgomery, Redding, CA**

8 fresh zucchini (about 7 inches long)

2 cups cottage cheese

2 eggs, well beaten

1/4 cup minced parsley

3 cloves fresh garlic, minced

Salt and white pepper to taste

Dash nutmeg

1/4 cup grated sharp Cheddar cheese

Slice zucchini in half lengthwise and parboil in boiling water for 10 minutes, until just tender but not soft. Drain, scoop out centers, and discard. Turn zucchini shells onto paper towels to drain and cool. When cool, place shells in an oblong buttered baking dish. Combine remaining ingredients and fill zucchini shells, dividing mixture evenly. Sprinkle each shell with cheese. Bake at 350 degrees F. for 15 or 20 minutes.

Makes 8 servings.

ARTICHOKE AND GARLIC FRITTATA

A frittata is nothing more than a flat Italian omelet to which, like an omelet, one can add almost any ingredient, such as meat, cheese, or vegetables, and topped with a generous sprinkling of freshly grated Parmesan cheese.

Recipe Contest entry: **Lisa G. Hanauer, San Francisco, CA**

15 to 20 cloves fresh garlic, peeled and coarsely chopped

1 large Bermuda onion, coarsely chopped

¼ cup olive oil

½ pound fresh mushrooms, sliced

2 (6-ounce) jars marinated artichoke hearts, drained and halved

8 to 10 eggs

4 ounces *each* Parmesan, Romano, and mozzarella cheese, freshly grated

⅓ cup Italian breadcrumbs

3 tablespoons Italian seasoning

2 tablespoons freshly ground pepper

2 teaspoons salt

Paprika

In a large skillet, sauté garlic and onions in oil until soft. Add mushrooms; sauté 5 minutes more. Add artichoke hearts; let mixture cool. In a large mixing bowl, beat eggs. Fold in cheeses, breadcrumbs, herbs, pepper, and salt. Combine with cooled artichoke and garlic mixture. Pour into two 9-inch cake pans. Sprinkle with paprika and bake at 375 degrees F. for 40 minutes, or until done.

Makes 10 servings.

GOURMET ALLEY VEGETABLE STIR-FRY

Central California's agricultural bounty is on display in this healthful and beautiful dish.

This recipe was created by the chefs at **Gourmet Alley**.

1/4 cup carrots

1/4 cup celery

1/4 cup yellow crooked neck squash

1/4 cup zucchini

1/4 cup broccoli

1/4 cup cauliflower

2 tablespoons oil

3 large cloves fresh garlic, minced

1/2 teaspoon salt

1/4 teaspoon pepper

Pinch red chili pepper

1/4 teaspoon *each* basil and oregano

1/4 cup dry white wine

1 tablespoon fresh parsley, chopped

Juice of 1/4 lemon

Cut carrots, celery, squash, and zucchini into 1/2 x 2-inch pieces. Break broccoli and cauliflower into small pieces. Heat oil until almost smoking. Add vegetables; stir to coat with oil. Add garlic, salt, peppers, basil, and oregano. Simmer 1 minute. Add wine and simmer 2 minutes, or until vegetables are cooked *al dente*. Add parsley and lemon juice, and serve immediately.

Makes 1 very generous serving.

RUBINO'S STUFFED MUSHROOMS

Rancher Jim Rubino shares his stuffed mushrooms that were one of the crowd favorites at the Festival's Gourmet Alley.

Recipe courtesy of **Jim Rubino, San Martin, CA**

I cup butter

¹/₃ cup crushed garlic

I pound grated Parmesan
    cheese

¹/₃ cup chopped parsley

50 large mushrooms

Melt butter, stir in crushed garlic, grated cheese, and parsley. Mix well. Brush mushrooms clean, remove stems. Stuff mushroom caps, smoothing the stuffing mixture. Place on a broiler pan, stuffing-side up, and broil until top turns golden brown. Serve out of the broiler.

Makes 50 stuffed mushrooms.

GARLIC PIE

An attractive, hearty dish that can be made ahead and baked just before serving.

Recipe Contest entry: **Kenneth Poppa, Gilroy, CA**

8 medium red potatoes, cooked

3 medium white onions, chopped

15 cloves fresh garlic, minced

3 to 4 tablespoons butter

$^1/_2$ teaspoon garlic salt

1 pound Italian sausage, removed from casings

1$^1/_2$ tablespoons oregano

1 tablespoon cumin

Salt and pepper to taste

2 eggs

1 cup milk

6 ounces mozzarella cheese, sliced

Paprika

Peel potatoes, reserving skins, and slice. Over low heat in a covered pan, cook onion and garlic in 2 to 3 tablespoons butter about 20 minutes. In a buttered 11-inch pie pan, make a crust out of the potato skins by pressing skins firmly to the pan. Sprinkle with garlic salt and dot with butter. Add sausage to onion-garlic mixture and brown. Add oregano, cumin, and salt and pepper and pour into piecrust. Beat eggs and milk together lightly and pour over sausage. Cover with cheese. Make another layer of sliced potatoes to form top crust. Dot with butter, sprinkle with paprika, and bake in 450-degree F. oven 20 to 30 minutes, until heated through and top is browned.

Makes 6 to 8 servings.

HAPPY HEART GARLIC "CHEESE" PIE WITH GARLIC-TOMATO SAUCE

Those on a low-fat, low-cholesterol diet need not sacrifice great garlic flavor. In fact, garlic has been credited by some in the medical community with lowering cholesterol.

Recipe Contest entry: **Carol Granaldi, Sacramento, CA**

2 egg whites

1 teaspoon fresh lemon juice

1 (14-ounce) package firm tofu, mashed well

1 cup chopped onion

4 tablespoons safflower oil

1/2 cup chopped cooked mushrooms *or* 1 (8-ounce) can, drained

1/3 cup minced fresh parsley

1/4 cup dry breadcrumbs

6 cloves fresh garlic, minced

1/2 teaspoon *plus* a pinch dried oregano

Salt and pepper to taste

1 (1-pound) can crushed tomatoes

1/2 teaspoon crushed dried basil

Dash cayenne pepper

In a large mixing bowl, beat egg whites until foamy; add lemon juice and tofu. Stir well. Sauté onion in 2 tablespoons oil until golden brown. Add to tofu mixture along with mushrooms, parsley, breadcrumbs, half the garlic, pinch of oregano, and salt and pepper to taste. Stir to mix thoroughly. Spray 8-inch glass pie dish with low-fat, no-cholesterol nonstick cooking spray. Pour mixture and spread evenly. Bake at 350 degrees F. for 30 to 40 minutes, until lightly golden in color or a knife inserted in the center comes out clean. Remove and let cool about 10 minutes. Meanwhile prepare sauce. Sauté remaining garlic in 2 tablespoons oil until golden, then add tomatoes, 1/2 teaspoon oregano, basil, cayenne, and salt and pepper to taste. Stir well and bring to bubbling. Reduce heat and simmer about 15 minutes. Cut pie into 4 wedges and top each with sauce.

Makes 4 servings.

MUSHROOM CRUST FLORENTINE PIE

Garlic devotees will likely want to add more garlic, and for a more subtle difference in flavor yogurt can be substituted for the mayonnaise.

Recipe Contest entry: **Jamie Schulte, Indianapolis, IN**

$^1/_2$ pound fresh mushrooms, chopped

3 tablespoons butter

$^1/_2$ cup dry breadcrumbs

1 $^1/_2$ cups shredded Swiss cheese

3 tablespoons flour

1 (10-ounce) package frozen chopped spinach, thawed and drained

6 crisp cooked bacon slices, crumbled

3 eggs

3 cloves fresh garlic, minced

3 scallions with tops, chopped

$^2/_3$ cup mayonnaise

1 teaspoon parsley

$^1/_2$ teaspoon pepper

Cherry tomatoes and hard-boiled egg slices for garnish

Parmesan cheese

Sauté mushrooms in butter, stir in breadcrumbs, spread and press evenly over the bottom and around the sides of a greased 9-inch pie pan to form the crust. Toss cheese with flour and add remaining ingredients. Mix well and fill crust with mixture. Bake at 350 degrees F. about 40 minutes. Garnish as desired and sprinkle lightly with Parmesan.

Makes 4 servings.

SOUPS, SALADS, AND DRESSINGS

GARLIC SOUP WITH CHICKEN

This chunky chicken broth is enriched with a purée made from a whole head of fresh garlic. What better prescription for good health and good eating?

Regional Winner 1984 Recipe Contest: **Carla Matesky, Canton, CT**

1 whole chicken, disjointed

2 carrots, minced

2 stalks celery, minced

1 whole onion, stuck with 2 cloves

1 whole head fresh garlic, broken into unpeeled cloves

Chopped fresh parsley

Salt and pepper to taste

10 cloves fresh garlic, peeled

4 tablespoons butter

2 tablespoons flour

Make fresh chicken broth by simmering chicken, carrots, celery, onion, garlic, parsley, salt and pepper in enough water to cover. When chicken is thoroughly cooked, remove, and skim fat from the broth. Simmer broth, reducing it until it is very rich. Remove unpeeled garlic cloves; squeeze cooked garlic from cloves and mash to make a purée. Discard skins. In a skillet, sauté the unpeeled cloves in butter. When lightly browned, add flour and a small amount of broth, and mix with a wire whisk until velvety. Pour this mixture into the remaining broth, add puréed garlic, and stir. Tear chicken into bite-sized pieces and add to the soup. Sprinkle with fresh parsley and serve.

Makes about 8 servings.

CREAMY GARLIC SPINACH SOUP WITH GARLIC CROUTONS

This soup has fabulous flavor, but be sure to serve it with homemade garlic croutons. Use day old sourdough French bread and combine with ¼ cup olive oil, 1 teaspoon each garlic powder and crushed dry parsley, ¾ teaspoon Hungarian paprika, and salt and pepper to taste. Cut bread into ½-inch cubes and work garlic-oil mixture into bread. Spread cubes in a shallow baking pan and bake at 325 degrees F. about 25 minutes. Store in a tightly covered container.

Third Prize Winner 1983 Recipe Contest: **Debra Kaufman, South San Francisco, CA**

1 large bunch spinach, stalks removed

4 cups chicken broth

2 large carrots, grated

1 large onion, chopped

8 cloves fresh garlic, finely chopped

½ cup butter

¼ cup flour

½ cup light cream

½ cup whipping cream

Salt and freshly ground pepper to taste

Sour cream (optional)

Garlic croutons

Chop spinach coarsely. Combine with chicken broth and carrots in 2- to 3-quart pot. Cook 5 to 10 minutes until carrots are tender and spinach wilted. Remove from heat. Meanwhile, sauté onion and garlic very gently over low to medium heat in butter, about 20 to 30 minutes. Onions should be very tender and translucent, but garlic should NOT be browned! Add flour and cook, stirring constantly, 5 to 10 minutes. Combine spinach/broth and onion/garlic mixtures in a food processor or blender in small batches. Purée until smooth. Clean pot and return soup to pot. Add cream, whipping cream, and salt and freshly ground pepper to taste. Heat until hot, but not boiling. Garnish with a dollop of sour cream and garlic croutons.

Makes 4 servings.

ESCAROLE-GARLIC SOUP WITH CHICK PEAS

This soup is a nutritious, satisfying, meatless main dish that's great served with toasty Italian bread.

Regional Winner 1983 Recipe Contest: **Peg Rhodes, Prescott, AZ**

1 bunch escarole (about
    1 pound)

4 tablespoons olive oil

5 to 6 medium cloves fresh
    garlic, finely minced or
    pressed

1 medium onion, sliced

2 quarts chicken broth
    (fresh *or* canned)

2 sprigs fresh parsley, chopped

1 (16-ounce) can garbanzos,
    drained

Freshly ground black pepper

2 cups cooked rice

Parmesan cheese, grated

Rinse and drain escarole to remove sand. Cut leaves crosswise into thin pieces. Heat olive oil in 4-quart saucepan. Sauté escarole, garlic, and onions in hot oil for 5 minutes. Add ½ cup of broth, cover, and simmer over low heat 25 to 30 minutes. (The leaves will shrink as they cook.) Add more broth if liquid is absorbed too quickly, to avoid burning. Add remaining broth, parsley, garbanzos, and pepper to taste. Cover and simmer 10 minutes longer. To serve, place ½ cup of the hot rice into a soup bowl and pour soup over. Pass Parmesan cheese and enjoy!

Makes 4 servings.

CALIFORNIA GARLIC SOUP FONDUE

This recipe offers an excellent way to use up leftover champagne.

Recipe Contest entry: **Beverly Szabo, Culver City, CA**

40 cloves (3 to 4 heads) fresh garlic, minced

3 tablespoons butter

2 (10³/₄-ounce) cans chicken broth

2 soup cans water

¹/₂ cup extra dry champagne

4 slices French bread

4 slices Gruyere cheese

Cayenne pepper

Minced chives

Sauté garlic in butter for 10 minutes, stirring often. Do not brown. Add broth, water, champagne, and simmer 5 minutes. Toast bread. Ladle soup into bowls. Float bread on top, sprinkle with cheese, and bake at 475 degrees F., uncovered, 25 minutes. Sprinkle with cayenne and chives.

Makes 4 servings.

HUNGARIAN PEASANT SOUP WITH SPAETZLE

Spaetzle are bite-sized dumplings and make this dish a meal in itself. The trick to developing the rich flavor is the slow cooking of the roux.

Recipe Contest entry: **Helen Headlee, South San Francisco, CA**

Soup

2 medium onions, chopped

6 to 8 cloves fresh garlic, minced

6 tablespoons vegetable shortening *or* 4 tablespoons vegetable shortening and 2 tablespoons bacon drippings

4 tablespoons flour

2 tablespoons Hungarian sweet paprika

3 cups boiling water *plus* 10 cups lukewarm water

1 cup minced parsley

5 to 6 carrots, sliced

4 to 5 potatoes, peeled and cut into large chunks

Salt to taste

Spaetzle

3 cups flour

3 eggs

½ to ¾ cup water

1 teaspoon salt

Sauté onions and garlic in 2 tablespoons melted fat until golden. Drain off excess fat. Remove garlic and onions, place in a bowl, and set aside. In the same pan, melt remaining 4 tablespoons of fat, gradually stirring in the flour and paprika. Continue cooking, stirring constantly, over low heat 4 to 5 minutes, being careful not to burn. Stir in boiling water, and cook another 3 to 5 minutes. Pour into a large pot filled with remaining water and stir in parsley. Bring to a boil, lower heat and add garlic, onions, carrots, and potatoes. Lower heat, cover, and simmer until vegetables are done and flavors are blended, about 30 minutes. Stir occasionally. Meanwhile, prepare dumplings and add to soup when ready to serve.

To make the spaetzle: Combine all ingredients. Dough will be very sticky. Bring a large pot of water to a boil and either coarsely grate dough into boiling water or place dough on a flat plate and with a sharp knife, scrape and slice small bite-sized pieces into the boiling water. When dumplings rise to top, drain and add to soup.

Makes 3 to 10 servings.

BARROOM CHOWDER

Although chowder originated in New England, it enjoys nationwide popularity today. There's a touch of the Southwest in this recipe that gives it an unusual flavor.

Recipe Contest entry: **Barbara Blosser, Alameda, CA**

¼ pound butter

1½ cups chopped onions *or* half leeks and half onion

3 cloves fresh garlic, minced

¾ cup chopped celery, including some leaves

¾ teaspoon *each* cumin (whole seed) and marjoram

⅓ teaspoon sage

⅓ cup flour

3 cups chicken stock *or* canned chicken broth

2 cups heavy cream

½ cup tequila

6 ounces shredded Cheddar cheese

2 tablespoons chopped cilantro

1 teaspoon red pepper *or* cayenne

½ teaspoon nutmeg

2 to 3 carrots, half shredded, half cut into ovals

Zest of 2 limes

1 pound fresh fish, your choice, cut in chunks

Melt butter in a large saucepan over moderate heat. Sauté onions and garlic for 5 minutes. Add celery and cook 5 minutes more. Stir in cumin, marjoram, and sage. Add flour; stir and cook 3 minutes or until bubbling. Add stock, cream, and tequila. Blend. Stir in cheese. Add cilantro, pepper, and nutmeg. Mix well. Add carrots and lime zest. Then add fish and cook until fish is tender, about 10 minutes. Serve with crackers or warm bread.

Makes 3 quarts of soup.

Garlic-Broccoli Soup

This rich and creamy soup is even better the day after it's made and may be served cold as well as hot. Add a little half-and-half the next day just before serving.

Recipe Contest entry: **Mrs. Jol Oberly, Memphis, TN**

12 cloves fresh garlic

1 large bunch fresh broccoli

4 tablespoons unsalted butter

3 tablespoons flour

1 teaspoon salt

¹/₂ teaspoon black pepper

2 cups milk

¹/₂ cup chicken broth

Half-and-half, as needed

Hungarian sweet paprika

Drop unpeeled garlic cloves into boiling water for 1 minute (30 seconds for small cloves); remove from water, peel, and mince. Cut broccoli into buds and stems, discarding woody portions, and cook in boiling water until tender. Remove and drain. Melt butter in a 2-quart saucepan. When butter begins to bubble, add garlic, stirring rapidly for a few seconds. Quickly add flour, salt, and pepper. Stir constantly for 1 minute. Add milk and chicken broth, stirring briskly with a wire whisk until sauce is thickened. In a blender or food processor, purée broccoli with a little sauce, adding remaining sauce until all broccoli is blended. Correct seasoning to taste and thin with half-and-half to proper consistency. Serve, sprinkled with Hungarian sweet paprika, if desired.

Makes 4 to 6 servings.

Garlic Tortilla Soup

This recipe was created by a disabled veteran who obviously enjoys cooking and eating well.

Recipe Contest entry: **Mike Conrad, Carson City, NV**

15 cloves fresh garlic

1 cup water

2 (10³/₄-ounce) cans chicken broth

Juice of 1 lemon

2 corn tortillas, cut into ¹/₂-inch pieces

2 egg yolks

Dash Tabasco

Pinch cumin

Peel garlic. In a blender, thoroughly mix garlic and water. Place in a 2-quart saucepan with broth and lemon juice; simmer 20 minutes. Add tortillas and cook an additional 10 minutes. Remove from heat and cool slightly. Slowly add egg yolks, stirring constantly. Reheat and add Tabasco and cumin.

Makes 4 servings.

Meatball Soup, California-style

This recipe was adapted from the "Sopa de Albondigas" so popular in Mexico. The Cheese-Butter, added to each serving at the very last moment, could be used to season and enrich almost any clear soup.

Recipe Contest entry: **Fresh Garlic Association**

4 large cloves fresh garlic

$^1/_2$ pound ground beef

1 large egg, beaten

1 $^1/_2$ teaspoons salt

2 teaspoons uncooked rice

$^1/_4$ cup finely chopped parsley

$^1/_2$ cup chopped onion

1 tablespoon oil

$^1/_2$ teaspoon lemon pepper seasoning

2 (10 $^1/_2$-ounce) cans beef broth

2 cups water

1 cup carrots, cut into 2 x $^1/_4$-inch strips

1 cup celery, cut into 2 x $^1/_4$-inch strips

1 (8 $^3/_4$-ounce) can garbanzos, undrained

1 (16-ounce) can stewed tomatoes

Cheese-Butter (see recipe)

Cheese-Butter

$^1/_2$ cup butter, softened

$^1/_2$ teaspoon pressed fresh garlic

2 tablespoons Parmesan cheese

1 tablespoon minced parsley

(Makes about $^1/_2$ cup)

Peel garlic. Mash or press 1 clove garlic. Combine with beef, egg, $^1/_2$ teaspoon salt, rice, and 2 tablespoons parsley. Shape mixture into 20 small meatballs and set aside. Chop or mash remaining 3 cloves garlic. Cook garlic with onion in oil over medium heat until soft, but not browned, in a covered 3-quart saucepan. Add remaining 1 teaspoon salt, lemon-pepper seasoning, broth, water, carrots, and celery. Bring to a boil. Drop in meatballs and simmer 20 minutes. Add undrained garbanzos, tomatoes, and remaining chopped parsley. Continue cooking 10 minutes longer. Ladle into large soup bowls and serve with a spoonful of Cheese-Butter.

To make the cheese butter: Combine all ingredients.

Makes 4 servings.

Cream of Artichoke Soup

This creamy soup depends partly for its seasoning on the herbs and spices in the marinade used on the artichoke hearts. Fresh garlic and onion provide just the right additional flavor balance.

Recipe Contest entry: **Fresh Garlic Association**

1 (6-ounce) jar marinated artichoke hearts

3 or more large cloves fresh garlic

$^1/_2$ cup chopped onion

2 tablespoons flour

2 (10$^3/_4$-ounce) cans chicken broth

1 cup half-and-half

Finely chopped parsley

Drain marinade from artichoke hearts into 2-quart saucepan. Crush garlic in a press, or mince and add to marinade. Add onion and cook, covered, for 10 minutes over low heat. Blend in flour. Slowly stir in 1 can of broth and heat to boiling. Boil 1 minute, or until mixture thickens. Turn artichoke hearts into a blender or food processor and add hot mixture, blending until smooth. Strain into a saucepan; add remaining can of broth and half-and-half. Heat just to serving temperature; do not boil. Sprinkle each serving with parsley.

Makes 4 servings, about 1$^1/_3$ cup each.

Garlic is a habit and a passion.

—*Chicago Sun-Times*

MIDDLE-EASTERN CARROT SALAD

A sweet and savory side dish to serve as an accent with meat and potatoes, rice, or pasta.

Recipe Contest entry: **Marion Marshall, Van Nuys, CA**

6 large carrots, peeled and cooked

3 to 4 cloves fresh garlic, minced

1 tablespoon salad oil

1 tablespoon paprika

1 tablespoon chopped parsley

1 teaspoon salt

1/2 teaspoon cumin

Juice of 1 large lemon *or* 1 1/2 tablespoons vinegar

Slice carrots into 1/4-inch rounds. Combine all other ingredients and add to carrots. Marinate 3 to 4 hours, or overnight.

Makes 4 servings.

SPINACH SALAD

A delicious salad with a good, garlicky bite to it!

Recipe Contest entry: **Lillie S. Marlork, Vallejo, CA**

1 pound fresh spinach, washed and dried

⅓ cup finely diced sharp Cheddar cheese

⅓ cup finely chopped celery

2 hard-boiled eggs, chopped fine

Vinaigrette

⅓ cup salad oil

5 cloves fresh garlic, crushed

2 tablespoons *each* lemon juice and vinegar

1 teaspoon sugar

1 teaspoon Dijon-style mustard *or* brown mustard

½ teaspoon salt

Dash pepper

Remove stems from spinach and tear leaves in to large bite-sized pieces. Combine in a salad bowl with cheese, eggs, and celery. Prepare vinaigrette dressing. Remove large pieces of garlic and pour dressing over spinach mixture. Toss lightly and refrigerate several hours before serving.

Makes 8 servings.

Eileen's Greens

Napa cabbage, also called Chinese cabbage, looks somewhat like a combination of Romaine lettuce and celery, but the individual leaves are pale green at the top and blanched white at the bottom. It is excellent in salads or cooked as a vegetable.

Recipe Contest entry: **Eileen Hu, Monterey, CA**

1 tablespoon sesame oil

3 cloves fresh garlic, minced

7 large leaves Napa cabbage, washed and cut into bite-sized pieces

½ onion, chopped

1 tomato, washed and sliced

2 tablespoons soy sauce

1 tablespoon sugar

Heat sesame oil in a skillet to 475 degrees F. Sauté garlic, being careful not to burn. Add cabbage and onion. Stir-fry for 1 minute. Add tomato, soy sauce, and sugar. Cook 2 minutes.

Makes 4 servings.

SCANDINAVIAN TRIPE SALAD

Long, gentle cooking brings out the flavor of this delicacy, which is prepared here in the Scandinavian manner with yogurt, sour cream, and vinegar, laced with the bite of fresh garlic. The cheesecloth sack, by the way, used for holding the garlic is not a necessity, only a convenience for retrieving the cloves for mashing.

Finalist 1982 Recipe Contest: **Alice Gray, Berkeley, CA**

I pound tripe

2 quarts cold water

¹/₂ lemon

I teaspoon salt

4 to 6 cloves fresh garlic, unpeeled

¹/₂ cup sour cream

¹/₂ cup plain yogurt

2 tablespoons white wine vinegar

I teaspoon sugar

¹/₄ teaspoon white pepper

Salt to taste

Minced chives

Rinse tripe in cold water, drain, and place in a large saucepan with 2 quarts cold water. Squeeze juice from lemon over tripe and drop in the peel. Add salt, and bring gently to a boil. Turn heat to low and simmer until tender, 20 minutes to 2 hours, depending on tripe. Meanwhile, tie garlic cloves in a cheesecloth sack, drop into boiling water, and cook until very tender, at least 20 minutes. Remove garlic, cool sufficiently to handle, and squeeze the garlic out of its peel into a medium-sized bowl. Add sour cream, yogurt, vinegar, sugar, and pepper, and mix well. Chill. When tripe is tender, rinse in cold water, drain, and cool. Cut into coarse or medium julienne strips, and combine with the dressing. Add salt to taste, mound into a serving bowl, and chill. At serving time, sprinkle with chopped chives. Serve as an hors d'oeuvre or as the main course of a light lunch.

Makes 4 servings.

EGGPLANT SALAD TRINIDADELISH

Serve this salad with cold roast chicken, crusty French bread, and fresh fruit for a beautiful summer meal.

Recipe Contest entry: **Thomas Davis, Waynesboro, MI**

1 large eggplant

6 ounces shell macaroni, cooked

1 medium tomato, chopped

1/2 cup olive oil

1/4 cup finely chopped garlic

1/4 cup freshly squeezed lime juice

4 tablespoons finely chopped parsley

2 tablespoons dry vermouth

1 tablespoon chopped green onion

2 teaspoons seasoned salt

1/2 teaspoon *each* oregano and basil

1/4 teaspoon freshly ground pepper

Lettuce

Wash eggplant; prick skin several times with a fork. Place on a baking sheet and bake at 350 degrees F. for 45 minutes, or until eggplant is tender. Cool; when cooled, peel and cut into 1/2-inch cubes. In a large bowl, combine eggplant, macaroni, and tomatoes. Prepare dressing by mixing all remaining ingredients and pour over eggplant-macaroni-tomato mixture. Cover, and refrigerate overnight. Serve on crisp lettuce leaves.

Makes 6 to 8 servings.

SHRIMPLY GARLIC POTATO SALAD

A hot, spicy dressing tops a combination of freshly boiled potatoes and garlic-sautéed shrimp.

Recipe Contest entry: **Bob Dixon, Santa Cruz, CA**

6 medium red potatoes

4 slices bacon, coarsely chopped

¹/₂ pound shrimp, cleaned and deveined

8 cloves fresh garlic, minced

¹/₃ cup white wine

2 tablespoons brown sugar

¹/₄ cup white wine vinegar

1 tablespoon German-style mustard

1 dill pickle, chopped

Salt and pepper to taste

Lettuce

Boil potatoes in their jackets 25 minutes, or until tender. Drain. In a large skillet, fry bacon until barely cooked, then add shrimp and garlic. Cook, stirring continuously, until shrimp have cooked through, being careful not to burn garlic. Remove bacon and shrimp, and set aside. Drain pan, and add wine and sugar. Simmer 1 to 2 minutes. Add vinegar and mustard, and simmer 1 minute longer. Set aside. Slice potatoes, still in their jackets, into a large bowl. Pour hot liquid over and combine. Add pickle, onion, shrimp, bacon, and salt and pepper to taste. Mix well and serve on crisp lettuce leaves.

Makes 4 to 6 servings.

LUCIA'S VEGETABLE SALAD

A very colorful salad that makes a crunchy contrast to Mexican food.

Recipe Contest entry: **Joyce Childs, Danville, CA**

$^1/_2$ cup vegetable oil

$^1/_2$ cup olive oil

$^1/_3$ cup wine vinegar

3 clove fresh garlic, finely minced

2 tablespoons capers (optional)

1 tablespoon finely minced parsley

1 tablespoon Italian seasoning

$^1/_2$ teaspoon salt

Pepper to taste

3 medium zucchini, cut into $^1/_2$-inch slices

1 (16-ounce) can medium ripe olives, not pitted, drained

1 basket cherry tomatoes

$^1/_2$ pound whole, small fresh mushrooms

2 to 3 (6-ounce) jars marinated artichokes, drained

Lettuce

Prepare dressing by combining first nine ingredients. In a large bowl, place zucchini, olives, tomatoes, and mushrooms and pour marinade over. Refrigerate 12 hours. Add artichokes, and combine. Arrange on a bed of lettuce in shallow bowl or serving platter. Drizzle marinade over.

Makes 6 to 8 servings.

Imagine a world without garlic. No spaghetti sauce. No veal parmigiana. No ratatouille. No Chinese cooking, Italian cooking, or Greek cooking. No fun.

—Savannah News

EGG SALAD WITH GARLIC DRESSING

For a change, use this egg-garlic dressing on a combination of vegetables such as green beans, peas, peppers, tomatoes, cucumbers, cauliflower, and broccoli.

Recipe Contest entry: **Betty Caldwell, Danville, CA**

6 cloves fresh garlic

I cup water

8 anchovies, including oil

6 tablespoons olive oil

2 tablespoons vinegar

I tablespoon capers

3 drops Tabasco *or* dash
   cayenne

Salt and pepper to taste

4 hard-boiled eggs

I pound watercress *or*
   I small head lettuce,
   shredded

Boil garlic in water 15 minutes until tender. Mash garlic with a fork to make a paste. Chop anchovies and combine in mixing bowl with garlic and all ingredients except eggs and greens. Mix well. Slice eggs in quarters. Tear greens into bite-sized pieces and arrange on a platter. Top with eggs and pour dressing over.

Makes 4 servings.

Garlicky Pasta Chicken Salad

In this recipe, slowly cooked garlic in rosemary-scented olive oil develops a rich, exquisite flavor.

Recipe Contest entry: **Mary Jane Himel, Palo Alto, CA**

6 whole heads fresh garlic

³/₄ cup olive oil

4 rosemary sprigs (optional)

¹/₄ cup fresh basil *or*
2 teaspoons dried

1 tablespoon fresh rosemary
leaves *or* 1 teaspoon dried

8 ounces corkscrew pasta,
cooked and drained

2 cups cooked chicken,
cut into strips

¹/₂ cup sliced green onion

¹/₂ cup freshly grated
Parmesan cheese

Salt and pepper to taste

²/₃ cup chopped walnuts

Lettuce leaves

Separate cloves of garlic; drop into boiling water for 1 minute. Drain and peel. Place peeled cloves in a small saucepan with oil and optional rosemary sprigs. Cook gently, covered, stirring occasionally, about 25 minutes, or until garlic is tender. Discard rosemary sprigs. Purée garlic with ¹/₂ cup of the olive oil, basil, and the rosemary leaves. Place pasta in a large bowl and add garlic purée, chicken, onion, Parmesan, salt and pepper. Mix thoroughly. Add more olive oil, if needed, to moisten salad. Let salad sit for 1 hour at room temperature or refrigerate, returning mixture to room temperature before serving. Toast walnuts in 375-degree F. oven for 10 minutes. Stir into the salad and serve over crisp, chilled lettuce.

Makes 6 servings.

GARLICKY GREEN GODDESS MOLD

As a spread for crackers, this molded salad also makes a great hors d'oeuvre.

Recipe Contest entry: **Julius Wolf, Culver City, CA**

2 envelopes plain gelatin

1/2 cup cold water

1 (8-ounce) carton plain yogurt

1 pint sour cream

1/4 cup *each* chopped parsley and chopped green onion

5 cloves fresh garlic, minced

2 tablespoons anchovy paste

1 tablespoon white vinegar

2 teaspoons Dijon-style mustard

1/2 teaspoon salt

1/8 teaspoon white pepper

1 medium cucumber, finely diced

1/4 cup celery, finely sliced

1/4 cup toasted, slivered almonds

8 lettuce leaves

8 cherry tomatoes

8 ripe olives

Sprinkle gelatin over water to soften. Stir over low heat until dissolved. Cool slightly. Pour into a blender with yogurt, sour cream, parsley, green onion, garlic, anchovy paste, vinegar, mustard, salt and pepper. Blend until smooth. Pour into a large bowl and fold in cucumber, celery, and almonds. Pour mixture into 1 1/2-quart mold that has been rinsed with cold water; chill until firm. Unmold onto lettuce leaves and garnish with tomatoes and olives.

Makes 8 servings.

MARIE'S AIOLI

This pungent mayonnaise can be used as a dip or salad dressing or to dollop on raw oysters, steak tartare, or seviche.

Recipe Contest entry: **Marie Spence, El Paso, TX**

2 tablespoons fine dry breadcrumbs

2 tablespoons wine vinegar

6 cloves fresh garlic, minced

3 egg yolks

$\frac{1}{2}$ teaspoon salt

Pinch white pepper

$\frac{1}{2}$ cup olive oil

1 tablespoon lemon juice

Soak breadcrumbs in vinegar; drain. Add garlic and mash to a smooth paste. Beat in egg yolks, one at a time, with salt and pepper. Then, beating vigorously, add $\frac{1}{4}$ cup olive oil, a few drops at a time. Continuing to beat, mix in the remaining oil by teaspoonfuls. Add lemon juice and mix thoroughly.

Makes about 1 cup.

BREADS, PASTA, AND RICE

MAHONY'S BRUSCHETTA

The Mahonys recommend keeping a bottle of olive oil in the refrigerator to which has been added 4 to 5 heads of peeled garlic. It's on hand when you want to make bruschetta, or you can add lemon juice for a salad dressing, to prepare oysters and linguine, or to add to pasta water for flavor, and to prevent boiling over.

Winner 1983 Recipe Contest: **Neil Mahony, Ventura, CA**

I loaf French *or* Italian bread without seeds

10 large cloves fresh garlic, peeled

³/₄ cup extra virgin olive oil

I¹/₂ cups whipping cream

¹/₂ cup grated Locatelli (hard Romano) cheese

¹/₂ cup grated Parmesan cheese

3 tablespoons butter

I tablespoon chopped parsley

Paprika

Cut bread diagonally in 1-inch slices but without cutting through the bottom crust. In a food processor or blender, chop garlic fine and, with the processor running, add olive oil to make a thin paste. Slather garlic paste onto cut surfaces and on top and side crusts of the bread. Place in a 350-degree F. oven, directly on the cooking rack with a pan on the rack below to catch drippings. Bake 10 to 12 minutes, until top is crispy looking. While bread is in the oven, heat whipping cream in a heavy saucepan. Do not boil. Using a wire whisk, slowly stir in cheeses so the sauce is absolutely smooth. Stir in butter; keep sauce warm until bread is ready. Wait until everyone is seated at the table. Then place crispy bread in a warmed, shallow serving dish with sides. Finish cutting through the bottom crust and pour sauce over. Sprinkle with parsley and paprika and serve *immediately*. This dish cools quickly.

Makes 6 servings.

GARLIC RAVIOLI

For those who enjoy making their own pasta, and who love garlic, this ravioli is irresistible.

Best Recipe Using Most Garlic 1983 Recipe Contest Winner: **Kellee Katzman, North Hollywood, CA**

5 large heads fresh garlic

2 cups chicken broth

11 tablespoons unsalted butter

1 1/2 cups ricotta cheese

1 cup grated Parmesan cheese

1 teaspoon garlic salt

2 sheets homemade pasta
    (about 5 x 24 inches each)

1 egg, slightly beaten

1/3 cup heavy cream

1/2 cup grated Romano cheese

Place heads of garlic in a shallow baking pan; pour chicken broth over and dot each head with 1 tablespoon butter. Cover and bake for 45 minutes, or until tender. Strain and reserve 1/3 cup liquid. Allow garlic to cool; then squeeze each clove into a bowl. Discard skins. Add ricotta, 1/2 cup Parmesan, and garlic salt, and mix thoroughly. Brush 1 sheet of pasta with egg and place garlic/cheese mixture in mounds (1 teaspoon each, about 2 inches apart). Place the second sheet of pasta over the first and press with your fingers around each mound. With a fluted pastry wheel, cut up into 2-inch square ravioli. Refrigerate 30 minutes. Bring a large pot of water to a boil. Just before the water begins to boil, start the sauce. In a frying pan, melt remaining 6 tablespoons of butter, add cream, and reduce slightly. Add reserved 1/3 cup liquid and reduce to a sauce consistency. When the water reaches a rapid boil, drop ravioli in and boil 3 to 5 minutes. Remove ravioli with slotted spoon and transfer directly into the reduced sauce. Sprinkle with remaining Parmesan and Romano cheeses.

Serves 4 to 6 as a first course.

GARLIC CLOVE BREAD

This sensational savory garlic bread is quick and easy and attractive to serve. If you prefer, you can bake it in two 9 x 6-inch loaf pans rather than a Bundt pan.

Regional Winner 1984 Recipe Contest: **Glen Peterson, Omaha, NE**

2 loaves frozen white bread dough, thawed

1/3 cup butter, melted and cooled to lukewarm

1/4 teaspoon basil

2 tablespoons chopped parsley

1 small onion, chopped

5 cloves fresh garlic, minced

Cut or snip pieces of dough, each about the size of a walnut. Place into a greased 10-inch Bundt pan. Combine the melted butter, basil, chopped parsley, onions, and minced garlic. Pour over dough. Cover and let rise until dough has doubled in size, about 1½ hours. Bake in a 375-degree F. oven until golden brown, about 30 to 35 minutes. Cool in the pan 10 minutes; remove from the pan and serve.

Makes 2 loaves.

Garlic: from Dracula to pasta, the herb reeks of history.

—Hackensack Record

HOT BRIE PASTA ALLA DIANE

The key to this recipe? Be sure the Brie is well ripened for a rich flavor.

Finalist 1983 Recipe Contest: **Diane Tarango, Hacienda Heights, CA**

I pound French Brie

½ cup olive oil

I cup fresh basil, cut into strips

4 large cloves fresh garlic, minced

4 tomatoes, seeded and cubed

½ teaspoon salt

¾ teaspoon freshly ground pepper

I pound linguine *or* angel hair pasta

6 ounces Parmesan, freshly grated

Remove rind from the Brie; cut cheese into irregular pieces. Combine with next 6 ingredients in a large bowl, and let stand for 2 hours at room temperature. Cook pasta until *al dente,* and drain. Toss hot pasta with Brie mixture.

Top with Parmesan cheese and serve at once.

Makes 4 to 6 servings.

KRUSTY GARLIC KUCHEN

This recipe is from a two-time finalist, a very creative cook whose entry won high praise from all who sampled it. It is also excellent served cold.

Finalist in 1982 Recipe Contest: **Patricia Bissinger, Livermore, CA**

Dough

1 envelope active dry yeast

1 1/2 cups warm water

3 cups unbleached flour

1 cup whole wheat flour

1/4 cup grated Parmesan cheese

1 egg, lightly beaten

2 tablespoons vegetable oil

1 teaspoon garlic salt

Garlic Topping

1 head (10 to 12 cloves) fresh garlic, minced

2 tablespoons vegetable oil

1 cup sour cream

2 eggs, lightly beaten

1/2 teaspoon salt

Minced chives *or* green scallion tops

Sprinkle yeast over warm water and let stand until bubbly. Meanwhile, measure all remaining dough ingredients into a food processor bowl. Add yeast mixture, and process just until dough forms a ball. Turn out onto a floured surface, and knead until dough is soft and no longer sticky. Shape into a ball. Place in a greased bowl, cover, and let rise in a warm place while preparing the topping.

To make the garlic topping: Peel and mince garlic cloves. Sauté 3 to 5 minutes in oil over low heat, until soft but not browned. Remove from heat and cool slightly, then combine with sour cream, eggs, and salt. Press dough into the bottom and up the sides of a greased 10 x 15 x 1-inch pan, forming a rim around the edges. Crimp the edge. Spread Garlic Topping evenly into the pan and sprinkle with minced chives. Bake at 400 degrees F. for 20 to 24 minutes until edges are well browned, and creamy garlic topping is light golden. Serve slightly warm, cut into strips as bread, or as an appetizer.

Makes 8 to 10 servings.

SOUTHERN CALIFORNIA'S BEST BREAD IN THE WEST

The chile, garlic, and Cheddar filling flavor combination brought this braided bread to the Contest finals.

Finalist 1982 Recipe Contest: **Rita Phister, Riverside, CA**

Bread

1 envelope active dry yeast

¼ cup warm water

½ cup milk

2 eggs

¼ cup soft butter

3 tablespoons sugar

1½ teaspoons salt

1½ teaspoons ground comino

3½ cups all-purpose flour

Green Chile Filling (see recipe below)

½ cup grated Cheddar cheese

Green Chile Filling

1 large onion, chopped

8 cloves fresh garlic, chopped

1 tablespoon butter

2 cups grated Cheddar cheese

1 (7-ounce) can diced green chiles

In the large bowl of an electric mixer, dissolve yeast in warm water. Blend in milk, eggs, butter, sugar, salt, and comino. Blend in 2 cups flour, 1 cup at a time. Beat on medium speed for 3 minutes, scraping bowl often. With a heavy duty mixer (or with a wooden spoon), blend in remaining flour to make a soft dough. Turn out onto a floured board, and knead until smooth, 5 to 10 minutes. Place in a greased bowl, turn over, and cover. Let rise in a warm place until dough has doubled in size, about 1½ hours.

Meanwhile, prepare Green Chile Filling. When dough has risen, punch down and turn out onto floured board. Roll to a 9 x 30-inch rectangle. Crumble filling over dough to within 1 inch of the edges. Starting on one long side, roll up tightly. Moisten edge with water and press dough firmly to seal. Using a floured sharp knife, cut the roll lengthwise in half. Carefully position the halves with the cut sides up. Loosely twist the two halves together, keeping the cut sides up. Transfer to a greased and floured baking sheet; shape into a 10-inch wreath. Pinch the ends firmly together. Let rise in a warm place, uncovered, until puffy, about 45 to 60 minutes. Bake at 375 degrees F. for 15 minutes. Sprinkle with ½ cup Cheddar cheese and bake 5 minutes longer, until browned.

To make the green chile filling: Sauté onion and garlic in butter until soft, but not browned. Cool. Mix in 2 cups Cheddar and chiles. Cover and chill.

Makes one 10-inch twist.

FETTUCCINE GARLI-MARI

A zesty calamari sauce using two heads of fresh garlic tops this rich, creamy fettuccine concoction.

Second Prize Winner 1982 Recipe Contest: **Byron Rudy, Livermore, CA**

2 heads (about 30 cloves)
    fresh garlic

2 pounds calamari

4 1/2 tablespoons butter

1 tablespoon olive oil

1/4 cup chopped parsley,
    packed finely

2 tablespoons dry white table
    wine

12 ounces fettuccine

1/2 cup heavy cream

2 1/2 ounces freshly grated
    Parmesan cheese

Press garlic cloves. Clean calamari, filet, and cut into 1/4-inch strips. Sauté garlic in 1 1/2 tablespoons butter and olive oil, stirring often, until soft and golden. Add calamari and cook over medium-low heat, turning often, until strips curl. Reduce heat, add wine and parsley, and cook 2 minutes longer. Meanwhile, cook fettuccine as package directs (coordinate cooking time with calamari, so both are done at once); drain. Melt remaining 3 tablespoons of butter in a hot serving bowl; combine butter, heavy cream, and Parmesan cheese. Add fettuccine and calamari, and mix with pasta forks. Serve immediately on warm plates.

Makes 6 servings.

FETTUCCINE ROBERTO

This Honorable Mention winner went on the following year to win Third Prize with another pasta recipe.

Honorable Mention 1983 Recipe Contest: **Robert J. Dyer, Gilroy, CA**

1 pound fettuccine

1/2 cup oil

1/4 pound butter

24 cloves fresh garlic, chopped

1 pound fresh jumbo shrimp, butterflied

1 cup chopped fresh parsley

2 cups chopped fresh mushrooms

1 cup chopped green onions

1 tablespoon red pepper

2 tablespoons flour

1/2 cup dry white wine

1 pint heavy cream

1 small (5-ounce) wedge Parmesan cheese, grated

Salt to taste

Cook noodles according to package directions in boiling water with oil. While noodles are cooking, melt butter in a large skillet over medium-high heat. Add chopped garlic and shrimp; cook until shrimp turns pink, but do not allow garlic to turn brown. Add parsley, mushrooms, onions, and red pepper; sauté for 1 minute. Add flour, mix thoroughly, and add wine. Simmer about 30 seconds, then add cream and heat through. Drain noodles, and add to sauce with the grated cheese. Fold in gently until noodles are well coated and cheese is melted. Salt lightly. If sauce is too thin, continue heating until sauce reduces to a creamy consistency. If sauce is too thick, add cream. Garnish with chopped parsley and additional grated cheese. Serve immediately.

Makes 4 servings.

There are many miracles in the world to be celebrated and, for me, garlic is among the most deserving.

—Leo Buscaglia

SPAGHETTACCINI CAROLINI

"If you live in the Garlic Capital of the World, it's only fitting that you should be a good garlic cook," claims Bob Dyer, who was also chairman of the very first Garlic Festival in 1979. Bob's colorful spaghetti dish attracted the judges with its stir-fried vegetables, succulent prawns, and plenty of garlic—24 cloves in all.

Third Prize Winner 1984 Recipe Contest: **Robert J. Dyer, Gilroy, CA**

I pound spaghetti

4 tablespoons oil

¹/₄ pound butter

24 cloves fresh garlic, peeled and chopped

I pound fresh jumbo shrimp, peeled and butterflied

I red bell pepper, thinly sliced

I bunch broccoli, cut into bite-sized spears

2 cups chopped fresh mushrooms

I cup chopped fresh parsley

I cup chopped green onions

I tablespoon dried red pepper

2 tablespoons flour

¹/₂ cup dry white wine

I pint heavy cream

I small (3-ounce) wedge Parmesan cheese, grated

Salt to taste

Cook noodles according to the package directions in boiling water with 2 tablespoons oil. Meanwhile, melt butter in a large skillet over medium-high heat. Add chopped garlic and shrimp; cook until shrimp turn pink, but do not allow garlic to brown. Set aside. In another skillet, over medium-high heat, stir-fry red bell pepper and broccoli in remaining 2 tablespoons oil. Cook until crisp-tender. Drain and set aside. Add mushrooms, half the parsley, onions, and red pepper to garlic and shrimp; sauté 1 minute. Add flour, mix thoroughly, and add wine. Simmer about 30 seconds, then add cream and heat through, stirring. Drain noodles and add to sauce with half the grated cheese. Toss gently until noodles are well coated and cheese is melted. Salt lightly. If sauce is too thin, continue heating until sauce reduces to a creamy consistency. If sauce is too thick, add cream. Gently toss in the stir-fried vegetables. Garnish with remaining chopped parsley and grated cheese. Serve immediately.

Makes 8 servings.

MAMMA'S SFEENJUNEE

Frank, Josephine, and Merrie Jo Fees, who entered their mother's recipe, describe this bread as easy, filling, wonderfully aromatic, and healthful. Mamma's special trick? Stick whole cloves into the dough.

Recipe Contest entry: **The Fees Family, Honolulu, HI**

1½ cups very warm water

1 envelope yeast

1 teaspoon sugar

5 tablespoons olive oil

4 cups flour

1 teaspoon salt

1 pound Italian sausage *or* Polish sausage, ham, or cooked pork

4 or 5 cloves fresh garlic

½ teaspoon Italian seasoning *or* oregano

½ cup black olives

Pour water into a large bowl, sprinkle in yeast, add sugar, and allow to sit for several minutes while it bubbles. Stir in 2 tablespoons olive oil. Combine flour and salt and add to yeast. Mix well. Knead about 10 minutes, cover, and set in a warm place to rise, 1 to 1½ hours. Meanwhile, remove skin from sausage and fry until cooked and crumbly. Drain off grease. Cut each garlic clove lengthwise into 6 slivers. Place in a cup and cover with remaining 1 tablespoon oil and seasoning. Cut olives in half and add to sausage. When dough has risen, pat into a greased 9 x 9 x 2-inch pan and evenly sprinkle the garlic-oil. Force sauce mixture down into the dough 1 teaspoon at a time. Bake at 375 degrees F. for 25 minutes, or until golden.

Makes 8 to 10 servings.

GARLIC FOCACCIA

Northern Italy's answer to pizza, this "cake which is not sweet" has many variations. To the basic focaccia, add artichoke hearts, preserved sweet red peppers, olives, mushrooms, cheese, or anchovies. Delicious hot from the oven, it also keeps well. For a stronger flavor, do not cook garlic. Add to the dough raw, then bake as usual.

Recipe Contest entry: **Carolyn Ragsdale, Paso Robles, CA**

½ cup chopped fresh garlic

⅓ cup olive oil

3 cups biscuit mix

1 cup milk *or* buttermilk

½ cup grated Parmesan
    cheese

Gently sauté garlic in oil until yellow, about 10 minutes. Pour through a strainer and reserve both garlic and oil separately. Combine biscuit mix, garlic, and milk. Pour a generous third of the oil into a 7 x 11-inch baking dish or pan. Spread the oil to coat the dish. Turn dough into the dish, pat out evenly with floured fingers. Pierce the dough every 2 inches with a knife or wooden skewer. Pour remaining oil over top of dough and spread evenly with floured fingers. Sprinkle Parmesan over the top and bake at 400 degrees F. for 24 minutes.

Makes 8 to 10 servings.

HOBO BREAD

This bread is baked in a coffee can. It's terrific with a rich hearty stew, or slice into rounds and pop into the toaster—that is, if there are any leftovers.

Recipe Contest entry: **Jacqueline McComas, Frazer, PA**

Butter (to grease two 1-pound
    coffee cans)

4 cups self-rising flour

¹/₂ cup grated Cheddar cheese

1 tablespoon dry basil *or*
    2 tablespoons fresh basil

¹/₄ cup butter

¹/₂ cup finely chopped fresh
    parsley

3 to 4 cloves fresh garlic,
    chopped

2 tablespoons honey

2 tablespoons chopped chives

¹/₂ cup milk

1 (12-ounce) can beer

Generously butter cans. In a mixing bowl, combine flour, cheese, and basil. In a saucepan, heat butter, parsley, garlic, honey, and chives until butter melts. Remove from heat and add milk. Add beer and *immediately* add to dry ingredients. Combine gently *only* until moistened. Divide dough evenly into the cans and bake at 350 degrees F. for 30 to 40 minutes, or until tops are very brown. Slice into rounds and serve with plenty of butter.

Makes 2 loaves.

PESTO LASAGNA FIRENZA

Pasta and pesto are natural together and especially tasty when combined in this delightfully different lasagna. For an excellent homemade pesto recipe, see Pesto Mushrooms, page 21.

Recipe Contest entry: **Florence Oefinger, Novato, CA**

6 to 7 lasagna noodles

2 cups pesto

¹/₂ cup half-and-half

4 large cloves fresh garlic, minced

2 tablespoons olive oil

1 tablespoon softened butter

1 pound Monterey Jack cheese, grated

3 tablespoons grated Parmesan cheese

Boil noodles as package directs. Rinse in cold water and drain. Mix pesto, half-and-half, garlic, oil, and butter in small bowl. Grease a loaf pan and spread several spoonfuls of pesto mixture over bottom. Cut noodles to fit pan and place in a single layer over the pesto. Spread a third of the pesto on top and sprinkle with a third of the Jack cheese. Repeat twice, ending with cheese. Sprinkle with Parmesan and bake at 350 degrees F. for 45 minutes.

Makes 2 to 3 servings.

It can be gentle, alluring and enticing, giving a marvelous subtle flavor to various dishes—a superb herb.

—Cincinnati Enquirer

NANCY AND J.R.'S PASTA

A crowd-pleasing pasta recipe that can be made with mild or super hot Italian sausage, as your taste dictates.

Recipe Contest entry: **Nancy Mertesdorf and Jeanette Renouf, San Jose, CA**

I pound hot Italian sausage

2 tablespoons oil

³/₄ pound fresh mushrooms, sliced

8 to 10 large cloves fresh garlic, minced

2 medium green bell peppers, julienned

I bunch green onions, chopped

¹/₄ cup dry white wine

4 tablespoons butter, softened

³/₄ pound fresh, thin, coiled spaghetti

6 ounces Parmesan cheese, freshly grated

Remove casing from sausage. Crumble and fry in a small skillet. Drain off excess fat and set aside. Heat oil in a large skillet or wok. Add mushrooms, half the garlic, peppers, onions, and wine. Stir-fry until crisp-tender. Meanwhile, add remaining minced garlic to butter and set aside. Cook pasta 4 to 5 minutes, or until tender. Drain well. Toss with garlic butter and Parmesan cheese, saving some for garnish. Add sausage and vegetable mixture to pasta and toss well.

Makes 12 servings.

LINGUINE CONTESSA

Served as a main course or side dish, as its name implies, this pasta has an aristocratic flair.

Recipe Contest entry: **Donna Richard, Bala Cynwyd, PA**

3 chicken bouillon cubes

1 ½ cups water

¼ cup olive oil

1 pound fresh mushrooms, sliced

¼ to ½ pound prosciutto, chopped

1 medium onion, chopped fine

4 cloves fresh garlic, minced

½ teaspoon black pepper

½ cup dry sherry

1 pound linguine

1 teaspoon salt

Freshly grated Parmesan cheese and parsley sprigs for garnish

Combine bouillon and water and boil several seconds, mixing thoroughly. Set aside. Heat oil in a large, deep pot and sauté mushrooms, prosciutto, onion, and garlic until onions and garlic are light golden brown. Add pepper, bouillon, and sherry. Bring to a boil, reduce heat, and simmer 10 minutes. Meanwhile, cook pasta in salted water until *al dente*. Drain pasta and combine with sauce. Serve hot with Parmesan cheese, garnished with small parsley sprigs.

Makes 6 servings.

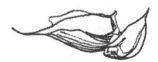

ITALIAN MEATBALLS AND SAUCE FOR SPAGHETTI

This recipe is intended to serve ten or more hungry people. You'll need a very large cooking pot, or you can use two smaller Dutch ovens. Just be sure to watch it while cooking to prevent scorching.

Recipe Contest entry: **Teresa Traversone, Tucson, AZ**

Meatballs

2 pounds lean ground beef

4 eggs, slightly beaten

³/₄ cup *each* grated Parmesan and Romano cheese

1¹/₂ cups dry breadcrumbs

1 cup milk

2 tablespoons chopped parsley

2 teaspoons salt

¹/₂ teaspoon garlic powder

Sauce

1 onion, chopped

¹/₂ cup olive oil

2 teaspoons instant minced garlic

3 (12-ounce) cans tomato paste

3 (15-ounce) cans tomato sauce

3 (29-ounce) cans whole tomatoes, chopped

2 teaspoons *each* oregano, garlic salt, and Italian seasoning

Combine first 8 ingredients and shape into meatballs. Coat a flat baking dish with nonstick cooking spray and place meatballs on pan. Bake at 350 degrees F. for 30 minutes, or until lightly browned. Meanwhile, prepare sauce.

To make the sauce: In a large heavy pot, brown onion in oil. Add minced garlic. Cook 1 minute longer. Add remaining ingredients including meatballs and simmer gently about 3 hours, or until sauce is proper thickness. Serve over cooked spaghetti. Sprinkle with additional grated Italian cheese, if desired.

Makes sauce for 10 or more servings.

GREEN RAVIOLI WITH GARLIC FILLING

What could be more appealing than homemade ravioli? Serve these with a creamy Alfredo sauce, or make a sauce of melted butter, chopped parsley, and minced garlic.

Recipe Contest entry: **James F. Benson, San Carlos, CA**

Filling

12 ounces Monterey Jack cheese

3 cloves fresh garlic

12 ounces grated Parmesan cheese

12 ounces dry breadcrumbs

Freshly ground pepper

1 cup dry white wine

3 eggs

Ravioli

1 (10-ounce) package frozen chopped spinach

2 cups unbleached white flour

1 tablespoon salt

1 tablespoon olive oil

2 eggs

Water as needed

In a food processor, grate Jack cheese. Remove cheese to a bowl. Process garlic. Add remaining dry ingredients and return Jack cheese to food processor container. Pulse until well mixed. Add wine to moisten, then add eggs and pulse until mixed.

To make the ravioli: Cook spinach according to package directions. Drain. When cool, press water out of spinach. Finely chop drained spinach. Add flour and salt and mix. Add oil and mix. Add eggs and mix. Add water until a ball of dough is formed. Place on a floured board. Knead until smooth and velvety. Place mixture in a plastic bag and set aside 1 hour. At this point, if you have a pasta machine, proceed to make the dough. If not, turn out only as much dough as you can handle at one time onto a floured board and roll until thin. On half the dough, spread some of the filling, then cover with the other portion of dough. With a ravioli rolling pin, or an 1/8-inch board, form ravioli, pressing rows of squares. Cut rows with a pastry cutter or knife. In a large pot of boiling water, cook ravioli until *al dente*. Drain, and serve with sauce of your choice.

Makes about 220 ravioli.

MANTI

An easy-to-fix casserole with the surprisingly rich and unusual lamb flavor.

Recipe Contest entry: **Cindy Mayron, Gilroy, CA**

1 (12-ounce) package large shell pasta

¾ pound ground lamb

1 tablespoon oil *or* butter

1 to 2 bunches green onions, minced

¼ cups chopped fresh parsley

4 cloves fresh garlic, minced

4 tablespoons butter

1 (10¾-ounce) can beef broth

1 (8-ounce) can tomato sauce

Cook pasta according to package directions. Drain and cool. Sauté lamb lightly in oil or butter; combine with onions, parsley, and garlic; mix well. Stuff shells with meat mixture. Butter bottom of a 3-quart baking dish with lid. Place shells in the baking dish and dot with butter. Cover, and bake in a 350-degree F. oven for 20 minutes. Combine broth and tomato sauce in a small pan and bring to a boil. Pour over manti and bake 15 to 20 minutes longer, until lamb is cooked and sauce thickens slightly.

Makes 4 to 6 servings.

BAKED MANICOTTI WITH MEAT SAUCE

An excellent pasta dish, the recipe makes enough filling to stuff 14 manicotti with some left over.

Recipe Contest entry: **Vicki Hilton, Santa Barbara, CA**

Sauce

1 pound lean ground beef

1 pound hot Italian sausage, casings removed

$^1/_2$ cup Italian breadcrumbs

$^1/_2$ cup virgin olive oil

3 cups chopped onion

8 to 10 cloves fresh garlic, chopped

$2^1/_2$ cups water

2 (1 pound 12-ounce) cans Italian tomatoes, undrained

9 ounces tomato paste

4 tablespoons chopped parsley

2 teaspoons *each* dried basil and dried oregano

$1^1/_2$ tablespoons *each* sugar and salt

$^1/_2$ teaspoon pepper

Filling

2 pounds ricotta cheese

8 ounces mozzarella cheese, chopped

$^1/_3$ cup grated Parmesan cheese

1 tablespoon chopped parsley

2 eggs

1 teaspoon salt

$^1/_2$ teaspoon Italian seasoning

$^1/_4$ teaspoon pepper

Freshly grated Parmesan cheese for garnish

Place beef and sausage in a skillet and brown thoroughly. Drain off grease, add breadcrumbs and blend with meat. Set aside. In hot oil in an 8-quart pot, sauté onion and garlic 3 to 5 minutes. Add remaining sauce ingredients and mix. Chop tomatoes into smaller pieces as they cook. Bring to a boil, reduce heat, and add meat mixture to sauce. Simmer, covered, stirring occasionally, 1½ hours. Cook manicotti according to package directions; parboil only. Drain and set aside. Meanwhile, combine all ingredients for filling and mix well with a wooden spoon. After manicotti has cooled and dried, stuff them with a spoon, being careful not to tear them. Set aside. In a large 8- to 10-quart casserole dish, spread a thick layer of sauce. Neatly place stuffed manicotti close together onto sauce. Add remaining sauce until casserole is nearly full. Sprinkle with about ¼ cup Parmesan cheese. Bake, covered, at 350 degrees F. for 45 minutes, or until bubbly; uncover and continue baking for another 10 to 15 minutes.

Makes 10 to 12 servings.

Garlic-Cheese Mostaccioli

Originated by a finalist in the 1982 Recipe Contest, he recommends serving it with his recipe for Tomatoes a la William, found on page 39.

Recipe Contest entry: **Bill Scales, Gilroy, CA**

1 (12-ounce) package
   mostaccioli

20 cloves fresh garlic, minced

1 large yellow onion, minced

4 tablespoons butter

Freshly ground black pepper

1½ pounds Colby cheese,
   grated

½ cup dry white wine

¼ pound mozzarella cheese,
   grated

¼ cup chopped fresh parsley

Prepare mostaccioli according to package directions, using a little olive oil in water. Drain. Keep warm in a shallow, ovenproof baking dish. Sauté garlic and onion in 2 tablespoons butter. Add pepper and set aside. Melt remaining 2 tablespoons butter in the top of a double boiler, add grated Colby cheese, and stir in wine. When cheese has melted, combine with garlic-onion mixture and pour over mostaccioli. Sprinkle with grated mozzarella and parsley; place on middle rack of the oven and broil 1 to 2 minutes.

Makes 10 servings.

SPINACH FETTUCCINE WITH ARTICHOKE SAUCE

A great pasta dish to serve with Thirty-Clove Chicken on page 178.

Recipe Contest entry: **Karen Harmatluk, San Francisco, CA**

2 (6-ounce) jars marinated artichoke hearts, drained, reserving marinade

3 tablespoons butter

I cup sliced mushrooms

³/₄ cup chopped walnuts

4 cloves fresh garlic, minced

3 tablespoons minced fresh basil *or* I tablespoon dried

I cup ricotta cheese

³/₄ cup Parmesan cheese

¹/₂ cup heavy cream

I (10-ounce) package spinach fettuccine

Coarsely chop artichoke hearts. Melt butter with reserved marinade in a skillet. Sauté artichokes, mushrooms, walnuts, garlic, and basil just until tender. In a blender, purée cheeses and cream. Mix well with artichoke mixture. Cook fettuccine according to package directions until *al dente*. Pour sauce over, toss to mix well, and serve at once.

Makes 6 servings.

There is no such thing as a little garlic.

—San Diego Union-Tribune

PASTA TERESA

This tasty combination of artichoke hearts, tomatoes, garlic, and thin spaghetti makes a great meal-in-a-hurry.

Recipe Contest entry: **Geoff Berkin, Los Angeles, CA**

1 whole head garlic, peeled

3 tablespoons *each* chopped fresh basil and oregano

4 medium tomatoes

³/₄ cup olive oil

2 thick slices bacon

2 (9-ounce) packages frozen artichoke hearts, thawed and drained

³/₄ pound spaghettini

4 ounces grated Parmesan cheese

Salt and pepper to taste

In a blender or food processor, purée garlic, basil, and oregano. Slice each tomato into 8 to 10 thin wedges, then slice wedges in half. Heat oil in a large skillet, add garlic purée and onion slices, and sauté over medium heat about 2 to 3 minutes. Remove onion and discard. Add tomatoes and artichoke hearts to skillet and gently mix. Lower heat and stir occasionally while pasta cooks. Cook pasta according to package directions until *al dente*. Drain. With a slotted spoon, remove tomatoes and artichoke hearts from the skillet to the bowl. Add drained pasta to skillet and toss to coat with oil. Add Parmesan cheese and toss, then salt and pepper. Divide pasta onto four plates, then top with equal portions of tomatoes and artichoke hearts.

Makes 4 servings.

TWO PEAS-IN-A-PASTA

Garbanzos and green peas make for a colorful presentation and a richly creamy flavor.

Recipe Contest entry: **Mrs. J. Rhodes, Prescott, AZ**

5 cloves fresh garlic, minced

6 tablespoons olive oil

1 (10-ounce) package frozen peas

1 (16-ounce) can garbanzos, drained, reserving liquid

1 teaspoon *each* dried basil and salt

1 pound fettuccine *or* linguine

¹/₂ cup half-and-half

¹/₂ cup grated Parmesan cheese

¹/₄ pound mozzarella cheese, grated

In a 10-inch skillet, cook garlic in olive oil until golden but not brown. Add frozen peas and garbanzos, basil, and salt. Lower heat, cover, and simmer 10 minutes. Meanwhile, cook pasta according to package directions. Drain. In a large serving dish, gently mix cooked pasta with half-and-half, Parmesan, and mozzarella. Pour cooked mixture over all, gently mixing through. Add reserved liquid if more moist pasta is desired.

Makes 4 to 6 servings.

PASTA VERDE WITH SPINACH AND ALMOND SAUCE

This recipe makes a delicious side dish for grilled chicken or fish.

Recipe Contest entry: **Carole L. Rutter, Hayward, CA**

1 bunch spinach *or* 1 (10-ounce) package frozen spinach

¼ cup coarsely chopped fresh parsley

¼ cup *each* grated Romano and Parmesan cheese

¼ cup vegetable oil

2 tablespoons butter

1 ounce blanched almonds

4 or more cloves fresh garlic

¼ cup boiling water, plus extra on hand

1 pound spaghetti

Parmesan cheese and chopped parsley for garnish

Wash spinach, remove stems, and chop leaves coarsely. Cook in a small quantity of boiling salted water until tender, or cook frozen spinach according to package directions. Drain. Place spinach in a blender with next six ingredients. Blend to a smooth paste. Add boiling water, and blend again for a few seconds. Extra water may be added to achieve desired consistency. Cook spaghetti according to package directions. Drain. Pour sauce over spaghetti and toss well. Garnish with extra Parmesan cheese and parsley, if desired.

Makes 4 to 6 servings.

PATCHWORK CALICO PASTA

Zucchini, broccoli, tomatoes, and toasted pine nuts bring unusual flavors, colors, and textures to this healthy dish.

Recipe Contest entry: **Cynthia Kannenberg, Brown Deer, WI**

4 zucchini, sliced diagonally (about ³/₄ pound)

2 cups broccoli flowerets

¹/₂ cup pine nuts

3 fresh tomatoes

I pound spaghetti

¹/₄ cup olive oil

I tablespoon minced garlic

I chile pepper (optional)

Salt and pepper to taste

¹/₂ cup half-and-half *or* heavy cream

¹/₄ cup butter

¹/₂ cup grated fresh Parmesan cheese

Blanch zucchini in boiling water for 1 minute; remove. Blanch broccoli for 3 to 4 minutes in boiling water. Drain. Peel and chop tomatoes. Toast pine nuts in 350-degree F. oven 5 to 10 minutes, being careful not to burn. Cook spaghetti as package directs until *al dente*. Drain. Heat oil in a skillet; add garlic, zucchini, broccoli, tomatoes, chile peppers, and salt and pepper. Cook briefly, stirring. Add drained spaghetti, cream, butter, cheese, and nuts. Discard chile pepper. Toss and serve immediately. Garnish with additional cheese, if desired.

Makes 6 to 8 servings.

FUSILI CON AGLIO, OLIO, PEPERONCINO E ZUCCHINI

This spicy pasta dish is also delicious chilled and served as a pasta salad.

Recipe Contest entry: **Laurie P. Farber, Sacramento, CA**

1 zucchini, ends trimmed and coarsely chopped

²/₃ cup olive oil

4 cloves fresh garlic

1 fresh jalapeño pepper, stem and seeds removed

1 tablespoon *each* fresh basil, thyme, and oregano *or* 1 teaspoon dried

Dash *each* black pepper, cayenne pepper, and salt

1 (16-ounce) can cannellini beans, drained and rinsed

1 pound fusilli

Grated Parmesan, Romano, asiago, *or* pecorino cheese (optional)

Garlic powder (optional)

In a food processor or blender, combine zucchini, oil, garlic, jalapeño pepper, basil, thyme, oregano, black and red peppers, and salt. Pulse until chopped but not puréed. Pour into a small saucepan and simmer over low heat, about 5 minutes, stirring occasionally. Add drained and rinsed beans; simmer 5 minutes more until beans lose a bit of moisture. Meanwhile, cook pasta according to package directions. Drain and pour sauce over, topping with grated cheese and a sprinkling of garlic powder, if desired.

Makes 4 servings.

SAUSAGE AND RICE, SWISS-STYLE

The caraway seed, frequently used in European cooking, adds distinctive flavor to the dish. To serve six, use 1¹/₂ pounds sausage, 1 cup rice, and 2 cups stock.

Recipe Contest entry: **Christine Ammer, Lexington, MA**

2 tablespoons vegetable oil

1 cup chopped onion

3 or more cloves fresh garlic, minced

1 pound Polish (Kielbasa) sausage, cut into 1-inch pieces

1¹/₂ cups chicken stock *or* chicken broth

³/₄ cup rice

1 teaspoon caraway seed

Salt and pepper to taste

In a large skillet, heat oil and cook onion and garlic until onion is soft. Add sausage and cook, stirring, 2 minutes. Stir in remaining ingredients. Bring to a boil, reduce heat, and cover. Simmer about 30 minutes, or until rice is done and liquid has been absorbed.

Makes 4 servings.

HOLLISTER HOT RICE

This family favorite is so popular, the judges were told, it's usually prepared in double quantities..

Recipe Contest entry: **Christy Funk, Hollister, CA**

2 cups long grain rice

6 or more cloves fresh garlic, minced

¹/₂ cup butter

2 (7-ounce) cans whole green chiles

¹/₄ pound Jack or Cheddar cheese

2 (10¹/₂-ounce) cans beef consommé (gelatin added) *plus* 2 consommé cans hot water

Sauté rice and garlic in butter in a skillet over medium heat about 3 minutes. Divide rice mixture in half, spreading half on the bottom of a 13 x 9 x 2-inch baking dish. Wash chiles in cool water. Slice cheese into strips and insert into whole chiles. Place stuffed chiles on rice mixture and spread remaining rice over. In a bowl, mix soup and hot water thoroughly; then pour over rice and chiles. Cover tightly with foil to keep rice from drying out. Bake at 375 degrees F. for 40 to 50 minutes.

Makes 6 servings.

...under the pot lids of exciting ethnic cuisines garlic has sneaked back into town. The uppity little bulb is ever emerging as the prime seasoning in favored recipes. Suddenly it's chic to reek.

—*Town and Country*

California Pilaf

This recipe, made in a slow cooker, couldn't be easier for hard-working home chefs.

Recipe Contest entry: **E. Saavedra, Denver, CO**

2 pounds ground beef

2 ¹/₂ cups water

2 (8-ounce) cans tomato sauce

1 ¹/₃ cups long grain rice

²/₃ cup sliced ripe olives

1 green bell pepper, seeded and chopped

1 small onion, chopped

3 cloves fresh garlic, minced

2 ¹/₂ teaspoons salt

¹/₄ teaspoon pepper

Brown beef in a skillet; drain off fat. Place beef and all remaining ingredients in a 4-quart slow cooker. Stir well. Cover and cook on low for 5 to 6 hours, or on high for 3 hours.

Makes 6 servings.

GARLIC DILL RICE

A savory accompaniment for roasted or broiled meats.

Recipe Contest entry: **Charles Valdes, Sacramento, CA**

3 to 4 cloves fresh garlic, minced

3 tablespoons olive oil

I cup rice

I (14½-ounce) can chicken broth

I teaspoon *each* dried dill and cilantro

I teaspoon salt

½ teaspoon onion powder

Sauté garlic in hot oil until golden. Add rice and sauté 4 to 5 minutes over high heat. Add broth and seasonings. Bring back to a boil, cover, and simmer over low heat 30 minutes. Fluff rice and allow to stand, uncovered, 5 minutes.

Makes 4 to 6 servings.

MAHONY'S RICE

This colorful dish was developed by the winner of the 1983 Recipe Contest for Mahony's Brushetta (see page 91). Neil suggests serving it with barbecued meats and a good Gewürztraminer. He also advises that it can be made in the morning, refrigerated, and reheated just before serving.

Recipe Contest entry: **Neil Mahony, Ventura, CA**

5 strips lean bacon, diced

1 medium onion, diced

1 medium green bell pepper, diced

8 cloves fresh garlic, chopped

1 cup long grain white rice, rinsed in cold water

1/3 cup *plus* 2 tablespoons soy sauce

1 2/3 cup water

1 (8-ounce) can button mushrooms, drained

1/3 pound cooked cocktail shrimp, fresh not canned

1 (4-ounce) jar diced pimentos, drained

6 tablespoons finely chopped fresh parsley

Fry bacon until crisp. Drain *thoroughly* and set aside. Fry onion, bell pepper, and garlic in bacon grease until onions are translucent. Drain *thoroughly* and add to bacon. In a saucepan, combine rice with soy sauce and water and bring to a boil. Cover tightly, reduce heat and simmer about 20 minutes, or until all liquid is absorbed. Remove lid and leave pan on very low heat to cook away any remaining moisture. After about 10 minutes, stir in bacon mixture, add half the parsley and almost all of the mushrooms, shrimp, and pimentos, saving some of each for garnish. Mix, and transfer to shallow serving dish and garnish, as desired. Serve at once.

Makes 6 to 8 servings.

PASTA CON PESTO ALLA PELLICCIONE

Paul Pelliccione, one of the head chefs of Gourmet Alley, shares his fabulous pasta con pesto as it was prepared for the Garlic Festival.

Recipe courtesy of **Paul Pelliccione, Gilroy, CA**

2 cups (packed) fresh basil leaves, washed and well drained

1½ cups or more grated Romano cheese

½ cup olive oil

½ cup melted butter

6 large cloves fresh garlic, crushed

1 pound spaghetti, cooked as the package directs

Place basil, 1 cup of the cheese, oil, butter, and garlic in a blender or food processor. Pulse the mixture, scraping the sides with a rubber spatula, and continue pulsing until you have a very coarse purée. Spoon 1 cup pesto sauce over freshly cooked spaghetti. Mix quickly with two forks. Add ½ cup cheese and mix. Serve with additional pesto sauce and cheese. Cover and refrigerate any leftover pesto up to one week. Or freeze in small portions. The surface will darken when exposed to air, so stir the pesto before serving.

Makes 4 servings as a main course, 6 to 8 servings as a side dish.

GOURMET ALLEY GARLIC BREAD

The heady aroma of this world-class garlic bread wafts irresistibly through the Alley for the duration of the Festival.

This scrumptious bread has evolved to perfection thanks to the chefs at **Gourmet Alley**.

1 cup butter

¹/₂ cup oil

3 cloves fresh garlic, minced

¹/₂ teaspoon pepper

¹/₄ teaspoon oregano

¹/₂ cup white wine

3 tablespoons fresh parsley

2 loaves sweet French bread

Melt butter in a saucepan. Add oil and garlic. Simmer over low heat for 1 minute. Add pepper, oregano, and wine. Bring to a boil. Add parsley. Remove immediately from heat; pour into a large baking pan. Cut loaves in half lengthwise. Toast on a grill or under a broiler until golden brown. Dip toasted halves, cut-side down, in butter mixture. Serve immediately.

Makes 4 half-loaves.

Robust bulb reputed to give strength, courage.

—Colorado Springs Gazette-Telegraph

CALIFORNIA GOURMET GARLIC LOAF

This recipe for a split loaf of French bread makes eight generous servings for crusty, cheesy, garlicky goodness.

Finalist 1982 Recipe Contest: **Leona Pearce, Carmichael, CA**

I long loaf sweet French bread

½ cup butter

6 cloves fresh garlic, crushed

1½ cups sour cream

2 cups cubed Monterey Jack cheese

¼ cup grated Parmesan cheese

2 tablespoons dried parsley flakes

2 teaspoons lemon pepper seasoning

I (14-ounce) can artichoke hearts, drained

I cup shredded Cheddar cheese

I (6-ounce) can pitted ripe olives

Tomato slices and parsley sprigs for garnish

I tablespoon sesame seeds

Cut French bread in half lengthwise. Place halves on a baking sheet covered with aluminum foil. Tear out soft inner portion of bread in large chunks, leaving crust intact. Melt butter in a large skillet, stir in garlic and sesame seeds. Add bread chunks and fry until bread is golden and butter is absorbed. Remove from heat. Combine sour cream, Jack cheese, Parmesan cheese, parsley flakes, and lemon pepper seasoning. Stir in drained artichoke hearts and toasted bread mixture; mix well. Spoon into bread crust shells and sprinkle with Cheddar cheese. Bake at 350 degrees F. for 30 minutes. Meanwhile, drain olives well. Remove bread from the oven; arrange olives around the edges of the bread and place tomato slices and parsley sprigs down center.

Makes 8 servings.

MEATS

GARLICIOUS LAMB ROLL-UPS

Stuffed lamb cutlets topped with a savory Olive Sauce and served over broad noodles makes a "garliciously" rich meal.

Regional Winner 1981 Recipe Contest: **HELEN MIZE, Lakeland, FL**

Stuffed Lamb

1 1/2 pounds lamb cutlets

1 1/2 teaspoons garlic salt

1/4 teaspoon black pepper

2 slices bacon

2 tablespoons chopped onion

1 cup soft breadcrumbs

1 tablespoon chopped parsley

1 1/2 teaspoons dried mint
    leaves, crumbled

1 teaspoon lemon juice

1 large clove fresh garlic

1/4 teaspoon crushed rosemary

1/4 cup flour

3 tablespoons butter

Olive Sauce (see recipe)

1 (8-ounce) package broad
    noodles

Olive Sauce

2 beef bouillon cubes

1 1/2 cups hot water

2 tablespoons butter

2 tablespoons flour

1 tablespoon tomato paste

1 bay leaf

1/3 cup sliced stuffed
    green olives

2 tablespoons dry sherry

Garlic salt and pepper
    to taste

Pound the lamb cutlets to flatten (or ask the butcher to do this for you). Trim off edges to make 8 rectangles, about 5 x 7 inches. Sprinkle with garlic salt and pepper. Finely dice lamb trimmings (½ to 1 cup) and bacon. Brown slightly in a skillet. Add onion, and cook until tender. Stir in breadcrumbs, parsley, mint, lemon juice, fresh garlic, and rosemary. Spread stuffing onto cutlets. Roll up, secure with toothpicks, and dredge in flour. Slowly brown on all sides in 3 tablespoons butter over moderately low heat. Continue cooking until meat is tender, about 30 to 40 minutes. Meanwhile, prepare Olive Sauce, and cook noodles in boiling salted water as package directs; drain well. Serve lamb rolls over noodles with sauce and crusty chunks of garlic bread.

To make the olive sauce: Dissolve 2 beef bouillon cubes in 1½ cups hot water. In a medium-size saucepan, melt 2 tablespoons butter and blend in 2 tablespoons flour. Slowly stir in broth. Cook, stirring until thickened. Add remaining ingredients, stir and season to taste.

Makes 4 servings.

LAMB SHANKS WITH BARLEY AND GARLIC

This hearty, award-winning dish requires 30 cloves of fresh garlic to achieve its robust flavor. If that's not enough for you, stud the lamb with slivers of fresh garlic before cooking.

Third Prize Winner 1982 Recipe Contest: **John Robinson, Granada Hills, CA**

Lamb

4 lamb shanks

$^1/_4$ cup *each* butter and olive oil

$^1/_2$ cup *each* red wine and water

$^1/_2$ teaspoon rosemary
(or more, if desired)

30 cloves fresh garlic, peeled

Barley

$^1/_2$ to $^3/_4$ pound fresh
mushrooms, sliced

$^1/_2$ cup butter

1$^1/_2$ cups pearl barley

2$^1/_2$ to 3$^1/_2$ cups beef bouillon

2 tablespoons mint jelly

In an ovenproof skillet with a tightly fitting lid, brown lamb on all sides in butter and olive oil. Remove lamb, stir wine and water into skillet and heat, scraping bottom and sides of skillet. Replace lamb and sprinkle with rosemary. Add at least 30 cloves of garlic. Place foil over top, then the tightly fitting lid to seal completely. Bake at 350 degrees F. for 1$^1/_2$ hours. Prepare barley.

To make the barley: Sauté mushrooms in $^1/_4$ cup butter and set aside. Brown barley in remaining $^1/_4$ cup butter until golden brown. Mix in mushrooms, turn into a casserole dish, and add 2$^1/_2$ cups beef bouillon. Cover, and bake 30 minutes at 350 degrees F. Add more bouillon as needed, about 1 cup, and cook, uncovered, until liquid is absorbed and barley is done. To serve, arrange lamb shanks around edges of serving platter. Add garlic cloves to barley and heap into the center of the platter. Stir mint jelly into the remaining liquid, cook 3 to 5 minutes, and spoon over lamb.

Makes 4 servings.

CHAD'S GARLIC LAMB

More than a seasoning, garlic is a major ingredient in this dish. Chad recommends pouring a hefty glass of wine before starting to separate and peel the 30 heads of garlic. It will help to sustain you through the task.

Regional Winner 1982 Recipe Contest: **Chad Reott, West Hollywood, CA**

1 leg of lamb (about 6 to 7 pounds)

30 heads of fresh garlic cloves, separated and peeled

1 large onion, peeled

Garlic powder

Onion powder

Italian seasoning

¹/₂ gallon dry red wine

3 tablespoons cornstarch

Coarsely chop 10 to 12 cloves garlic and onion; set aside. Spread remaining whole garlic cloves over bottom of a roasting pan. With a metal skewer, pierce holes in the lamb (lengthwise). Stuff holes with chopped garlic and onions (a chopstick simplifies this step). Sprinkle lamb generously with garlic powder, onion powder, and Italian seasoning. Nestle lamb onto the bed of garlic cloves and pour enough wine over to reach a depth of ¾ inch. Roast lamb, uncovered, in a 325-degree F. oven about 30 minutes per pound, or until lamb is done to your liking. Remove lamb to a warm platter. Pour contents of pan into a blender and liquefy. Transfer to a saucepan. Mix 1 cup wine with cornstarch and add to liquid; heat until sauce is thickened. Carve lamb and pour some sauce over. Pass remaining sauce.

Makes 6 servings.

RACK OF LAMB BREADBIN

Plan ahead if you want to try this lamb dish, as it is best if marinated for about four days in the refrigerator. For extra browning, run it under the broiler for a few minutes just before serving.

Regional Winner 1982 Recipe Contest: **Rowena Bergman, Toronto, Ontario, Canada**

1 rack of lamb (about 5 to 6 pounds)

³/₄ cup cloves fresh garlic, peeled

¹/₂ cup olive oil

Juice of 4 lemons

3 heaping tablespoons dry mustard

2 heaping tablespoons bouquet garni

1 heaping tablespoon tarragon

Ask your butcher to cut through the shinbone, so meat can be carved into individual chops at the table, and trim off fat around ends of the ribs and around the kidney area. Combine garlic and all remaining ingredients in a food processor or blender and process until liquefied. Place roast in a large plastic bag, add marinade, coating the roast, including the cuts made by butcher. Seal bag and refrigerate at least 2 days. To roast, remove from the bag, place lamb in a roasting pan, and insert a meat thermometer into the thickest part of the meat. Roast at 450 degrees F. until thermometer registers "medium" for beef. The lamb will be medium-rare at this point. If you prefer well-done lamb, follow thermometer accordingly.

Makes 4 servings.

How anything as small and delicate looking as a clove of garlic can have such an impact on food never ceases to amaze.

—*Los Angeles Times*

PORK AND CHICKEN LOS ARCOS

The pork and chicken are marinated in advance to give the meat a rich flavor. Eat the garlic cloves with your fingers by pinching the tasty clove out of its skin.

Finalist 1983 Recipe Contest: **Raymond G. Marshall, Pasadena, CA**

3 pounds pork shoulder

2 pounds chicken thighs

40 cloves fresh garlic, unpeeled

1 tablespoon salt

1 cup vinegar

2 tablespoons lemon juice

8 bay leaves

1/2 teaspoon *each* fresh ground
pepper and caramel coloring

4 whole cloves

6 very thin slices fresh ginger

2 tablespoons vegetable oil

2 tablespoons plain gelatin

2 (11-ounce) cans peeled lichees

1 cup toasted pumpkin seeds

Cut pork into 1½-inch cubes. Bone chicken and cut each thigh into 3 to 4 pieces. To prepare marinade: peel, chop, and mash 4 cloves garlic in salt to make a paste. Add vinegar, lemon juice, bay leaves, pepper, caramel coloring, cloves, and ginger; mix well. Pour over pork and chicken and marinate 6 to 8 hours in the refrigerator, stirring frequently. Remove pork and chicken from marinade and reserve marinade. Sauté pork in oil for 20 minutes. Add chicken and sauté 20 minutes more. Then add the remaining 36 unpeeled garlic cloves. Add gelatin to reserved marinade to soften, adding a little water, if necessary. Stir marinade well, add to pork and chicken and cook about 30 minutes, or until meat is done and tender. Add drained lichees and seeds to pot. Let cook about 5 minutes to heat through and serve, preferably with steamed rice.

Makes 8 servings.

FLANK STEAK OLÉ

Don't worry about small chunks of tamale which might fall out of the steak rolls; they add an interesting texture to the sauce.

Finalist 1982 Recipe Contest: **Sandy Hoiles, Sunnyvale, CA**

1 flank steak (about 2 to 2 1/2 pounds), tenderized

10 cloves (about 1 head) fresh garlic

1/2 teaspoon salt

1/4 teaspoon pepper

1 teaspoon chili powder

1 (15-ounce) can tamales, papers discarded and sauce reserved

1/4 cup flour

2 to 3 tablespoons olive oil

1 (8-ounce) can tomato sauce

1 cup red wine

1/3 cup grated Parmesan cheese

Stretch steak gently, without tearing it, into a rectangular shape. Press 3 cloves garlic over meat, sprinkle with salt, pepper, and chili powder. Crumble tamales over steak, spreading to within 1 inch of edges. Roll up steak, making a firm roll, but not too tight, and tie with string at intervals, or secure with skewers. Dust with flour, shaking off excess. Heat oil in a Dutch oven or a heavy skillet with a lid, and brown roll on all sides over medium-high heat. Reduce heat to low. Pour tomato sauce over roll. Measure wine into the tomato sauce can and pour into the tamale can with its reserved sauce. Press remaining 7 cloves of garlic into this sauce, stir, and pour *around* the roll—not over it. Cover, and simmer until tender, about 2 to 2 1/2 hours. Remove from heat and remove string or skewers, disturbing the topping as little as possible. Sprinkle with cheese and return to low heat. Cover, and cook until cheese melts, about 20 minutes. Place the roll on a serving platter and cut into 1-inch slices. Pass sauce separately in a gravy boat or bowl.

Makes 4 servings.

VEAL GARLIC CHOP

Cooking for one? Pamper yourself with this delicious, garlic-laced veal chop with peppers.

Regional Winner 1983 Recipe Contest: **David Lindley, Union City, CA**

1 veal chop (about 14 ounces)

1 tablespoon crushed black peppercorns

Salt to taste

2 tablespoons butter

1 tablespoon olive oil

1 green bell pepper

1 red bell pepper

1 medium onion, peeled

6 cloves fresh garlic, minced

1 teaspoon finely chopped fresh parsley

Rub veal chop all over with crushed black peppercorns and salt to taste. In a heavy skillet, combine butter and oil until hot, but not smoking; add veal and reduce heat to medium. Brown the veal about 7 minutes, turn, and brown the other side. Meanwhile, remove seeds and membrane from bell peppers. Slice peppers and onion into julienne strips and add to the veal. Add a pinch of salt. Spread garlic evenly over the chop; cover, and cook about 10 minutes, stirring vegetables occasionally, until tender. To serve, arrange bell peppers and onion on a plate, top with the veal chop, and sprinkle with parsley.

Makes 1 generous serving.

Now the pungent bulb is back in favor, its nervy aroma drifting from the best kitchens to enhance many a little dinner party.

—*Town and Country*

Rabbit with Lentils

This two-time finalist specializes in hearty dishes made with grains and legumes. In this casserole, rabbit is paired with lentils and finished with the fruity sweetness of apple.

Finalist 1983 Recipe Contest: **John Robinson, Granada Hills, CA**

8 rabbit legs and thighs

Flour, as needed

1/2 cup butter, unsalted

1/4 cup olive oil

1 pound dried lentils

Salt and pepper to taste

Cayenne

1/2 pound thick-sliced bacon, cut into 2-inch pieces

20 to 25 cloves fresh garlic, peeled

1 1/2 cups thickly sliced fresh mushrooms

1/2 cup gin (with strong juniper berry flavor)

1/2 cup crabapple jelly

1/2 cup finely chopped parsley

1 can spiced red crabapples

1 bunch watercress

Dredge rabbit in flour and sauté over moderately high heat in 1/4 cup each butter and olive oil until brown on all sides. Remove rabbit and save pan with drippings. Cook lentils according to package instructions, but stop when slightly underdone. Drain lentils, stir in remaining 1/4 cup butter, and season with salt, pepper, and a generous dash cayenne. Line the bottom of a heavy casserole with tightly fitting lid with bacon. Layer lentils on top of bacon, add rabbit pieces, heap garlic around rabbit, and cover all with remaining lentils. Spread mushrooms on top and seal casserole with aluminum foil. Then, carefully cover casserole with its lid and bake at 350 degrees F. for 1 1/2 hours. Remove rabbit from casserole and arrange on a serving platter. Stir balance of casserole ingredients together and mound in the center of the platter. Heat pan with reserved drippings over moderately high heat, add gin, and stir until thoroughly deglazed. Add crabapple jelly, and stir until completely combined. Remove from heat, add parsley, and stir. Pour over rabbit. Garnish with crabapples and watercress.

Makes 4 servings.

JOHN'S NEAPOLITAN BEEF ENTRÉE

A southern Italian-style casserole that bakes with a crusty cheese topping and plenty of garlic flavor.

Recipe Contest entry: **Vicki Leffler, Independence, KY**

¹/₃ cup chopped onion

4 or more cloves fresh garlic, crushed

1 cup diced carrots

¹/₂ cup diced celery

¹/₄ cup salad oil

1¹/₂ pounds ground chuck

1 (16-ounce) can tomatoes

1 (6-ounce) can mushrooms, drained

1 (6-ounce) can tomato paste

¹/₂ cup sherry

1 teaspoon salt

¹/₂ teaspoon *each* pepper, dried oregano, and basil

8 ounces shell macaroni, cooked

1 (10-ounce) package frozen spinach, drained

1 cup grated sharp Cheddar cheese

¹/₂ cup buttered breadcrumbs

Parmesan cheese

Sauté onion, garlic, carrots, and celery in oil for 5 minutes. Add meat; cook and stir until lightly browned. Add next 8 ingredients. Simmer, uncovered, 1¹/₂ hours. Add macaroni and spinach; mix well. Turn into a 2-quart casserole. Top with Cheddar cheese and breadcrumbs. Bake, uncovered, at 325 degrees F. about 30 minutes, or until hot. Serve with Parmesan cheese.

Makes about 8 servings.

POT ROAST WITH GARLIC-DILL SAUCE

Dill pickle is one ingredient that gives this pot roast its piquant flavor. The addition of sour cream at the last minute helps to blend all the flavors into a rich, delicious sauce.

Recipe Contest entry: **Alexis Ann Smith, Bowie, MD**

1 boneless rolled beef rump roast (about 4 pounds)

1 teaspoon *each* salt and white pepper

¹/₂ teaspoon ginger

2 tablespoons bacon grease

¹/₂ cup dry white wine

Water

2 cups sliced mushrooms

4 cloves fresh garlic, minced

2 tablespoons *each* chopped dill pickle and chopped pimento

1 tablespoon chopped fresh parsley

³/₄ teaspoon caraway seed

2 tablespoons cornstarch

2 tablespoons dill pickle juice

³/₄ cup sour cream at room temperature

Sprinkle roast with salt, pepper, and ginger. In a Dutch oven, brown roast on all sides in hot grease. Add wine, cover, and simmer 2½ hours. Remove roast and keep warm. Skim fat from drippings, add enough water to make 1½ cups of broth in the pan. Add mushrooms, garlic, pickle, pimento, parsley, and caraway seed. Blend cornstarch with pickle juice and 2 tablespoons water. Add to pan. Cook, stirring, 5 minutes. Gradually blend in the sour cream. Heat through. Slice meat and serve with sauce.

Makes 6 to 8 servings.

Pot Roast Gilroy

Red wine and coffee—yes, coffee— help to create an abundance of rich brown gravy to serve with this pot roast over noodles, potatoes, or rice.

Recipe Contest entry: **Sylvia Barber, Danville, CA**

8 or more cloves fresh garlic

1 large onion

1 lean chuck roast (about 4 to 5 pounds)

1 cup dry red wine, preferably Burgundy

3 tablespoons oil

2 cups strong black coffee

1 bay leaf

Water

Salt and pepper to taste

2 tablespoons cornstarch

Peel garlic and onion and slice lengthwise into strips. Using a sharp knife, pierce the roast all the way through in several places. Stuff 2 to 3 slivers of garlic and 1 to 2 slices of onion into each slit. Place roast in an enamel, glass, or stainless steel pan and pour wine over. Cover, and refrigerate 24 to 48 hours, turning occasionally. Drain wine and reserve. Pat roast dry. Brown roast in hot oil in a large pot until very well browned. Drain off excess fat and discard. Add coffee, bay leaf, and enough water mixed with the reserved red wine to make 2 cups. Bring to a boil, then simmer 2 to 3 hours. Add salt and pepper during last 30 minutes of cooking. Remove meat and bay leaf from the pot. Mix cornstarch and water to make a thin paste. Add to simmering liquid and stir until thickened. Return meat to gravy, or slice and pour gravy over. Serve with mashed potatoes, noodles, or rice.

Makes 6 to 8 servings.

GARLIC SPARERIBS

Whether they are served as a main course or as an appetizer, these steamed ribs are outstanding. If you don't have a steamer, simply place ribs on a rack in a large covered pot or wok.

Recipe Contest entry: **Erline Dair, South San Francisco, CA**

3 pounds spareribs

8 cloves fresh garlic, finely chopped

6 tablespoons *each* soy sauce and oyster sauce

3 tablespoons dry sherry

Hot chili oil (optional)

Chopped green onions (optional)

Chop spareribs into bite-sized pieces. Cover with water and bring to a boil. Parboil spareribs 10 minutes. Drain, and rinse with cold water. Combine remaining ingredients, except chili oil and green onion. Mix with spareribs and place on a heatproof dish on a rack in a steamer. Steam 45 minutes. Garnish with green onion and serve with optional chili oil, if desired.

Makes 4 servings.

Gilroy is an example of well-managed small-town living that could have remained a secret... except for a festival it hosts annually called the Gilroy Garlic Festival.

—*Ford Times*

Tenth Anniversary Ribs

This recipe was developed in honor of a tenth wedding anniversary. It combines the lightly sweet flavor Jill likes and the peppery spiciness Ron enjoys.

Recipe Contest entry: **Jill Goddard and Ron Kraus, Newhall, CA**

8 cloves fresh garlic, minced

3 (8-ounce) cans tomato sauce

3 small onions, minced

2 cups red wine

1 (4-ounce) can diced green chiles

5 tablespoons maple syrup

3 tablespoons *each* soy sauce and red wine vinegar

2 tablespoons prepared mustard

1 tablespoon Worcestershire sauce

1 teaspoon celery seed

¹/₂ teaspoon black pepper

¹/₄ teaspoon *each* cayenne pepper and smoke salt

3 to 4 pounds beef *or* pork ribs

Combine all ingredients, except ribs, in a large enamel kettle. Bring to a boil, reduce heat and simmer, uncovered, 1 hour, stirring occasionally. Meanwhile, place ribs in a deep pot; cover with water. Bring to a boil, cover, and simmer 45 minutes to 1 hour to remove fat and tenderize ribs. Remove ribs to a shallow baking pan, pour sauce over, and bake 30 minutes at 350 degrees F., turning and basting occasionally.

Makes 2 to 3 servings.

Spareribs Gilroy

Chinese Five Spice Powder brings an Asian-fusion flair to these easy-to-make spareribs.

Recipe Contest entry: **Lori Allen, Tacoma, WA**

2/3 cup soy sauce

1/3 cup maple syrup

8 cloves fresh garlic, minced

3 tablespoons peach brandy

2 teaspoons *each* Five Spice
Powder and ground ginger

2 pounds spareribs

In a bowl, combine all ingredients, except ribs, and mix well. Place ribs in a shallow dish, pour mixture over, and turn ribs to coat. Marinate 2 hours, turning the ribs about every 15 minutes. Place ribs in one layer on a rack over a shallow baking pan in 450-degree F. oven. Pour boiling water to 1-inch in the bottom of the pan. Brush ribs with marinade, and bake 30 minutes. Turn ribs, brush with more marinade. Reduce heat to 350 degrees F. and continue baking 45 minutes, turning ribs once more. Transfer ribs to a cutting board and chop into 3-inch lengths.

Makes 4 servings.

SUMPTUOUS SPARERIBS

Cooking time will vary according to how meaty the ribs are. Check every half hour and test for tenderness. When ribs are fork-tender, they are ready to serve.

Recipe Contest entry: **Dorothy Jenkins, Livermore, CA**

4 pounds pork spareribs, cut into single serving-sized pieces

10 cloves fresh garlic, peeled

1 onion, chopped fine

1 tablespoon butter

1 cup *each* catsup and water

6 tablespoons brown sugar

1/4 cup chopped celery *or* 1 tablespoon celery salt

4 tablespoons lemon juice

2 tablespoons *each* vinegar and Worcestershire sauce

1 tablespoon ground mustard

1/4 teaspoon cayenne pepper

Place spareribs in a baking pan with a lid. Split 6 cloves garlic at the top to release flavor and sprinkle over ribs. Cover pan, and bake at 350 degrees F. for 1 hour. Pour off the grease. Mince remaining 4 cloves of garlic and fry with onions in butter until onion is transparent, being careful not to burn garlic. Add all remaining ingredients and pour over ribs evenly. Cover, and bake at 350 degrees F., basting every 30 minutes and checking with a fork for doneness. May take up to 2 hours. Bake, uncovered, for the final 30 minutes.

Makes 4 servings.

The herb of mirth and medicine, remedy and rancor will be abundant in all its forms.

—1001 Home Ideas

Angela's Steak Milanese

An inexpensive version of a classic Italian dish that substitutes thinly sliced round steak for veal.

Recipe Contest entry: **Angela Vannucci, Fremont, CA**

1 lean round steak (³/₄ pound) sliced thin

1 egg

¹/₄ cup water

1 cup plain breadcrumbs

¹/₄ cup olive oil

5 to 6 cloves fresh garlic

Pinch of salt

2 dried hot chile peppers, finely chopped

Peel of ¹/₂ lemon, cut into thin strips

2 sprigs fresh rosemary without stems

2 (8-ounce) cans tomato sauce

Dip steak in egg that has been beaten with water. Dredge meat in breadcrumbs. Pour olive oil into a large skillet to ¹/₈ inch and heat until very hot. Brown steak quickly in oil, turning once, until golden, adding more oil if needed. Remove from skillet and drain on paper towels. Wipe out skillet and pour about ¹/₁₆ inch oil. Heat to very hot. Chop garlic and, with salt, chile peppers, lemon peel, and rosemary, add to hot oil; sauté briefly. Then add tomato sauce and meat. Gently cover meat with sauce, and simmer over low heat at least 30 minutes.

Makes 3 to 4 servings.

BUFFET MEAT LOAF

This recipe bakes in two loaf pans, making enough meat loaf for about six people. If there's any left over, it slices nicely when chilled.

Recipe Contest entry: **Terry Santana, Saratoga, CA**

3 pounds lean ground chuck

1/2 pound fresh spinach, washed and coarsely chopped

8 cloves fresh garlic, minced

2 cups soft breadcrumbs

1 large onion, chopped

1 tablespoon Madeira wine

2 teaspoons dried thyme

1 tablespoon salt

1 1/2 teaspoons pepper

1 teaspoon ground cumin

1/2 teaspoon crumbled rosemary

3 raw eggs

8 hard-boiled eggs, whole

In a large mixing bowl, combine ground chuck, spinach, garlic, breadcrumbs, onion, wine, and seasonings. Beat raw eggs lightly and add. Lightly toss all ingredients together. Using two 6-cup loaf pans, layer a quarter of the meat mixture into each pan. Place a row of 4 eggs down the center of each loaf. Cover eggs with remaining meat, smoothing the top. Place loaves on a baking sheet in 350-degree F. oven and bake 1 1/2 hours. Allow loaves to cool 10 minutes, then invert on a platter and serve.

Makes 6 to 8 servings.

QUICKIE CUBE STEAKS

Incredibly quick and easy and, best of all, "delicioso."

Recipe Contest entry: **Ann Laramee, Los Angeles, CA**

4 cube steaks

4 slices Monterey Jack cheese

4 cloves fresh garlic, minced

1 (4-ounce) can diced green chiles

Salt and pepper to taste

2 tablespoons oil *or* butter

On each cube steak, place 1 slice of cheese and top with garlic, chiles, salt and pepper. Roll up and secure with toothpicks. In a skillet, fry steaks in oil until meat is browned and cooked to desired doneness.

Makes 4 servings.

Driving north from San Juan Bautista you can usually count on abundant advance warning that you are approaching Gilroy. When the wind is blowing the right... way, the unmistakable aroma of garlic can be detected in the air for many miles around.

—*Michael Dorman*

Veal Fricasee with Garlic

A buffet dish that is definitely company fare, but why not treat the family, too?

Recipe Contest entry: **Susan Grossman, Tucson, AZ**

1 pound veal stew meat, cut in
$\frac{1}{2}$-inch cubes

6 tablespoons flour seasoned
with salt and pepper

3 tablespoons butter

2 tablespoons cooking oil

1 cup coarsely minced onions

3 large cloves fresh garlic,
minced *or* pressed

$\frac{1}{2}$ pound fresh mushrooms,
sliced thin

$\frac{1}{2}$ cup dry white wine

$\frac{1}{2}$ cup veal stock *or* chicken
stock

$\frac{1}{2}$ cup heavy cream

1 tablespoon minced fresh
parsley

Dredge veal in flour and shake off excess. Heat butter and oil in a heavy skillet, and brown veal in batches until golden. With a slotted spoon, remove veal to a platter and keep warm. Add onions, garlic, and mushrooms to the skillet, cover, and cook until onions are soft. Remove onion-garlic-mushroom mixture from the skillet with a slotted spoon and add to platter with the veal. Pour off any remaining butter or oil from the skillet and discard. Add wine and deglaze, scraping up all brown bits; cook 2 minutes. Return veal and vegetables to the skillet, add stock, cover and simmer 30 minutes, or until veal is tender and sauce has thickened. About 10 minutes before serving, add cream and simmer another 5 minutes, until sauce is thick. Pour veal and sauce onto a hot serving platter and sprinkle with minced parsley. Serve with egg noodles or rice.

Makes 4 servings.

CHOW YUK

On Chinese restaurant menus, this dish usually contains a variety of vegetables and this recipe is no exception. It also calls for "fresh Chinese noodles." If not available, substitute dried noodles or rice.

Recipe Contest entry: **Barbara Towe, Gilroy, CA**

1 flank steak (1 ¼ pounds)

½ cup soy sauce

6 cloves fresh garlic, peeled

3 tablespoons peanut oil

3 slices fresh ginger

½ pound fresh mushrooms, sliced

¼ pound fresh bean sprouts

¼ pound fresh sugar peas, blanched (optional)

1 (5-ounce) can water chestnuts, drained and sliced

1 green bell pepper, seeded and cut into slivers

1 medium tomato, cut into eighths

Fresh Chinese noodles, cooked and fried

Cut flank steak in half lengthwise; then slice each half diagonally into thin slices. Marinate in ¼ cup soy sauce and 3 sliced garlic cloves for 2 to 3 hours. Heat oil in a wok or large skillet. Stir-fry ginger and 3 whole garlic cloves, discarding both when lightly browned. Stir-fry meat quickly until brown, and add remaining ¼ cup soy sauce. Cover, and steam meat 45 seconds. Transfer meat to a platter and keep warm. To the liquid in the pan, add all the vegetables except the tomato. Stir-fry about 1 minute. Return meat to the wok and mix thoroughly with the vegetables. Add tomato wedges on top, cover, and cook 1 minute. Serve meat and vegetables with remaining liquid on top of Chinese noodles.

Makes 4 servings.

Veal Cutlet Parmigiana

For the best flavor, be sure to use an imported Italian Parmesan and grate it just before preparing the recipe.

Recipe Contest entry: **Carole A. Lake, Gilroy, CA**

4 veal cutlets, pounded
    very thin

Flour

4 large eggs, beaten

Plain breadcrumbs

¼ cup olive oil

½ cup butter

⅛ cup chopped chives

3 cloves fresh garlic, mashed
    and chopped fine

2½ cups marinara sauce

4 slices prosciutto

4 slices mozzarella cheese

Salt and pepper to taste

Grated Parmesan cheese

Dip cutlets into flour, then into egg, and then into breadcrumbs. Repeat. Sauté breaded cutlets for 6 minutes in oil and half the butter. Melt remaining butter and add chives and garlic. Set aside and keep warm. Pour a layer of marinara sauce on the bottom of a baking dish. Place cutlets on top of sauce and pour a little sauce over. Cover each cutlet with a slice of prosciutto; then pour garlic, chives, and butter over. Place a slice of cheese on top and lightly salt and pepper. Spoon remaining marinara sauce on top to cover meat. Sprinkle with grated cheese. Bake, uncovered, at 350 degrees F. for 20 minutes. Serve at once.

Makes 4 servings.

LAMB SHANKS, BASQUE-STYLE

This recipe was developed over thirty years ago and has been embellished and improved over the years to near perfection.

Recipe Contest entry: **M. Bernal, Morgan Hill, CA**

4 lamb shanks

¹/₂ cup *plus* 2 tablespoons
    salad oil

10 cloves fresh garlic

¹/₂ pound fresh mushrooms

¹/₂ cup to 1 cup chicken broth

¹/₂ cup dry red wine

1 cup navy beans

Salt and pepper to taste

¹/₂ cup chopped fresh parsley

¹/₄ cup wine vinegar

In a heavy Dutch oven, brown the lamb shanks in 2 tablespoons of salad oil. Remove lamb and reserve. Add 4 cloves garlic and mushrooms; brown well. Return lamb to the Dutch oven, add wine and ¹/₂ cup broth. Cook, covered, in 350-degree F. oven about 2 hours, adding more broth as needed, until meat falls from bones. Meanwhile, cook beans with 4 cloves of garlic in water to cover until soft. Drain and remove garlic. Remove bones from the lamb. Add beans and salt and pepper to cooked meat and heat through. Serve with a sauce made by combining ¹/₂ cup salad oil, 2 minced cloves of garlic, parsley, and vinegar.

Makes 4 servings.

GLORIA'S LAMB STEW

This is lamb stew with a difference—chile peppers, garlic, and fresh cilantro are the seasonings.

Recipe Contest entry: **Gloria Park, Los Gatos, CA**

1 cup fresh cilantro

1 whole head fresh garlic, peeled

2 to 3 fresh hot red *or* green peppers, seeded

1/2 cup olive oil

2 medium onions, finely chopped

4 pounds lean boneless lamb, cut into 1-inch cubes

Salt and freshly ground pepper to taste

2/3 cup fresh orange juice

1/3 cup lime *or* lemon juice

Water

2 pounds potatoes, peeled and sliced

1 pound fresh green peas, hulled *or* 2 packages frozen peas

In a blender or food processor, purée cilantro, garlic, and peppers; set aside. Heat oil in a casserole or Dutch oven and sauté onions until soft. Stir in cilantro mixture and cook for 1 to 2 minutes longer. Add lamb pieces and cook about 5 minutes, turning to coat with sauce. Season to taste with salt and a generous amount of pepper. Add orange and lime or lemon juice and enough water to cover, about 1 1/2 cups. If desired, this dish may be refrigerated at this point in order to solidify and remove any excess fat. Let stand to bring to room temperature before heating. Boil potatoes and peas separately in salted water until tender. Drain and add to casserole. Bring casserole to a simmer and cook just long enough to heat through.

Makes 4 to 5 servings.

Garlic: Eat it with someone you love.

—Fayetteville Observer

MARINATED GRILLED LEG OF LAMB

Menu suggestions from the chef to serve with the lamb: Baked Potatoes with Butter and Feta Cheese, Tomatoes and Sugar Snap Peas Vinaigrette, Homemade Sourdough Rolls, and Fresh Raspberries and Cream.

Recipe Contest entry: **Linda Nee, Keller, WA**

1 leg of lamb (about 7 to 9 pounds)

10 cloves fresh garlic, finely chopped

1 cup honey

1 cup soy sauce

1/3 cup dry sherry

Bone and butterfly lamb, or ask your butcher do this for you. In a small bowl, combine garlic, honey, soy sauce, and sherry. Place lamb in a large roasting pan or large shallow baking dish. Pour marinade over, cover with plastic wrap, and let stand at room temperature at least 12 hours or overnight. If desired, lamb can be marinated 3 or 4 days in refrigerator, but be sure to allow to come to room temperature before grilling. Grill lamb over hot coals to desired state of doneness. For rare, allow approximately 15 to 20 minutes per side. Let meat rest for 5 to 10 minutes before carving. If desired, heat remaining marinade and serve as sauce for the meat.

Makes 8 to 10 servings.

The best thing to do with garlic, of course, is to eat it.

—*San Francisco Chronicle*

ORANGE-GARLIC PORK CHOPS

The flavors of garlic, onion, and ginger combined with the tang of fresh orange help to transform pork chops into an exotic main course.

Recipe Contest entry: **Grace Maduell and Reid Brennen, San Rafael, CA**

6 pork chops

1 medium orange

6 cloves fresh garlic

½ small onion

¼ teaspoon powdered ginger

Pepper

1 to 2 tablespoons butter

Salt to taste

Remove fat from chops. Squeeze orange into a small bowl, keeping as much pulp as possible. Press garlic into orange juice. Using a garlic press, squeeze onion into orange-garlic mixture, being sure to remove onion skin. Add ginger and a pinch of pepper; stir well. Place chops in a shallow baking dish, cover with marinade, and let stand at least 45 minutes. Melt butter in a skillet with a lid. Remove chops from marinade, reserving marinade, and brown chops on both sides in butter. Cover with remaining marinade and cook, covered, for 10 minutes. Remove cover and cook until fork-tender. Add salt and pepper to taste.

Makes 6 servings.

SPICY CHOPS AND CABBAGE

Apples and cabbage are favorite ingredients in German cuisine. Combined here with garlic, they produce a deliciously different flavor blend.

Recipe Contest entry: **Margie Opresik, Phillips, WI**

4 pork loin chops, ³/₄-inch thick

3 cloves fresh garlic, peeled

4 tablespoons water

1 teaspoon salt

¹/₂ small bay leaf

3 medium apples, peeled, cored, and coarsely chopped

1 medium head cabbage, cored and coarsely chopped

¹/₂ small onion, chopped

¹/₄ cup sugar

2 tablespoons *each* vinegar and water

1¹/₂ teaspoons flour

Trim fat from chops; cook fat in a skillet to oil its surface. Discard fat; brown chops in the skillet. Add garlic, 2 tablespoons water, ¹/₂ teaspoon salt, and bay leaf; cover, and simmer for 30 minutes. Remove chops and discard garlic and bay leaf. To the skillet add apples and cabbage. Blend onion, sugar, vinegar and water, flour, and remaining ¹/₂ teaspoon salt. Cover, and simmer 5 minutes. Return chops to the skillet; cover, and cook 20 minutes until chops are fork-tender.

Makes 4 servings.

CHILE VERDE (MEXICAN STEW)

This dish is quite different from the classic Mexican dish of the same name, but is a very delicious adaptation. And it can be made ahead, stored in the refrigerator, and served the next day.

Recipe Contest entry: **Jeannine Johnson, Guerneville, CA**

1 pound beef stew meat (boneless chuck)

½ pound pork stew meat

2 large onions, chopped

6 cloves fresh garlic, minced *or* pressed

1 teaspoon *each* salt and powdered garlic

2 tablespoons olive oil

1 (4-ounce) can diced green chiles

3 (8-ounce) cans tomato sauce

Cut meat into 1-inch cubes. Place meat in a pot, cover with water, and add half the onion and half the garlic, salt, and powdered garlic. Cover, and simmer gently until meat is almost fork-tender. Remove cover, and continue cooking until meat is tender and liquid has boiled away. Meanwhile, in a separate saucepan, combine olive oil, remaining onion and garlic, chiles, and tomato sauce. Simmer about 10 minutes. Pour over meat, and bake 1 hour at 350 degrees F.

Makes 8 to 10 servings.

Indispensable garlic is lauded in Gilroy, where you can buy braids, (and) sample dishes.

—Sunset Magazine

CABALLERO CASSEROLE

Try this Southwest version of lasagna.

Recipe Contest entry: **Micky Kolar, Fountain Hills, AZ**

2 tablespoons cooking oil

2 cups chopped onion

1 red bell pepper, seeded and chopped

1 green bell pepper, seeded and chopped

3 cloves fresh garlic, minced

2 pounds lean ground beef

1 (16-ounce) can ready-cut tomatoes, drained

1 (4-ounce) can chopped jalapeño peppers, drained

2 tablespoons chili powder

2 teaspoons salt

1/2 teaspoon *each* ground cumin and oregano

1/4 teaspoon ground coriander

3 corn tortillas (10-inch diameter)

1/2 cup shredded Longhorn Cheddar cheese

1 ripe avocado, peeled and cut into 6 slices

1 cup sour cream

2 teaspoons minced parsley

Heat oil in a large, heavy skillet. Sauté onion and peppers until tender. Add garlic and sauté 2 minutes. Add meat and brown until crumbly. Add tomatoes, jalapeños, and spices, mixing well, and cook over medium heat until mixture is slightly thickened, about 5 minutes. Remove from heat. Oil a round 10 x 1 1/2-inch baking dish. Place 1 tortilla in the bottom of the dish, trimming to fit, if necessary. Spread a third of the meat mixture over the tortilla. Repeat layers, ending with meat. Bake in a preheated 400-degree F. oven for 15 minutes. Sprinkle with cheese and return to the oven for 5 minutes. Arrange avocado slices in sunburst pattern in the center of the casserole. Place a spoonful of sour cream in the center, sprinkle with parsley, and serve with additional sour cream, if desired.

Makes 6 servings.

GARLIC FESTIVAL STEAK SANDWICHES

Chef Lou Trinchero and his team of cooks served 700 pounds of top sirloin, 250 pounds of green peppers, and 750 loaves of French bread during the Festival. Lou reworked his recipe down to feed four generously.

Recipe courtesy of **Lou Trinchero, Gilroy, CA**

8 bell peppers, seeded and quartered

1 medium-sized onion, chopped

3 cloves fresh garlic, minced

Salt and pepper to taste

Olive oil

1 top sirloin steak (about ³/₄ pound), barbecued *or* broiled to desired degree of doneness

6 French rolls, halved, and basted with garlic butter

Garlic Butter (see page 206 for recipe)

In a skillet, sauté peppers, onion, garlic, and salt and pepper in olive oil until tender. Brush rolls with garlic butter and heat in the oven, or toast lightly under the broiler or over the barbecue. Slice steak thin and place on the bottom half of a roll. Top with pepper-garlic mixture and the other half of the roll.

Makes 8 sandwiches.

OUR BEST WURST

This homemade salami recipe makes enough for fifty people when sliced as a snack.

Recipe Contest entry: **Bob and Sylvia Solterbeck, Hooks, TX**

10 jalapeño peppers, minced (optional)

5 cloves fresh garlic, minced

½ cup curing salt

4 tablespoons dry red wine

2 tablespoons brown sugar

1 tablespoon *each* chili powder, Italian seasoning, and coarse ground black pepper

1 teaspoon *each* ground cumin and oregano

5 pounds lean ground beef

Combine all ingredients, except beef, then mix into beef. Refrigerate mixture 24 hours to allow flavors to blend. Form into 4 rolls. Wrap in aluminum foil and bake in 225-degree F. oven 4 hours, turning every hour. Remove foil and place on a broiler pan or rack to allow excess liquid to drain. Then rewrap rolls and refrigerate or freeze.

Makes 4 (1-pound) salamis. Recipe may be doubled, if desired.

Now garlic is to Gilroy what Mardi Gras is to New Orleans.

—*Los Angeles Herald-Examiner*

POULTRY

STUFFED CHICKEN BREASTS A L'AIL

Although only three chicken breasts are used in this recipe, the skin from six is needed to wrap the six stuffed half breasts. Reserve the remaining chicken for another meal, or marinate and grill them when you prepare this recipe and freeze them to serve later.

Regional Winner 1983 Recipe Contest: **Mrs. Robert Soelter, Abilene, KS**

Chicken

6 whole chicken breasts

3 cloves fresh garlic, minced

1 1/2 cups Monterey Jack cheese, grated

Salt

Cracked black pepper

Nutmeg

1 jar marinated Brussels sprouts, drained

6 teaspoons capers

Basting Sauce (see recipe below)

Basting Sauce

3/4 cup dry white wine

3/8 cup olive oil

3 cloves fresh garlic, minced

1/2 teaspoon salt

Carefully remove skin from 6 chicken breasts and set aside. Bone chicken breasts. Cut three chicken breasts in half. Cover chicken with a sheet of heavy plastic wrap and pound with a wooden mallet until very thin. Combine garlic and cheese. Lightly sprinkle each chicken breast with salt and cracked black pepper. Place 1/4 cup garlic-cheese mixture on each breast to within 1 inch of its edge. Sprinkle with nutmeg. Cut Brussels sprouts in quarters and arrange evenly over chicken. Top with capers. Fold in sides of flattened chicken and roll to make neat packages, covering the stuffing well. Wrap each breast in a chicken skin, securing with toothpicks. Grill over charcoal 30 to 40 minutes, basting with sauce.

To make the basting sauce: Combine all ingredients and mix thoroughly.

Makes 6 servings.

101 GARLIC CHICKEN

When serving this recipe to guests, invite them into the kitchen to let them count as you place the garlic cloves around the chicken. They won't believe how sweet and delicious the cooked garlic will be until they eat it!

Best Recipe Using the Most Garlic Winner 1982 Recipe Contest: **Helen McGlone, Roseville, CA**

10 whole chicken breasts, split, boned, and skinned

Salt and pepper

2 cups champagne

101 unpeeled cloves fresh garlic

Place chicken in an ungreased 12 x 16-inch or 12 x 18-inch baking pan. Sprinkle with salt and pepper and pour champagne over. Place garlic cloves around and between chicken pieces. Cover pan with foil. Bake at 350 degrees F. for 1½ hours. Remove chicken to a large serving platter and place garlic around chicken.

Makes 20 servings.

GARLIC-CHICKEN FILO ROLLS

The prosciutto will give this dish a smoky richness that substituting with ham will not. Also, be sure to keep the filo dough moist—as you work with it, cover it with a dampened towel.

Finalist 1982 Recipe Contest: **Mary Ann Himel, Palo Alto, CA**

2 heads fresh garlic

½ cup dry white wine

Juice of 1 lemon

¼ teaspoon salt

1 pound boned, skinned
    chicken breasts

6 sheets filo dough

¼ cup butter, melted

2½ ounces thinly sliced
    prosciutto *or* 3 slices
    boiled ham, halved

2 cups grated Swiss cheese

Separate garlic into cloves and drop into boiling water. Simmer 1 minute, drain, and peel. Bring wine, water, lemon juice, and salt to a simmer in a large saucepan. Add chicken and garlic. Cook at a bare simmer, turning occasionally, just until chicken is cooked. Remove chicken and continue cooking garlic until tender; drain. Cut chicken into large chunks and divide into 6 portions. Lay out 1 filo sheet, brush half with butter, and fold in half crosswise. Brush with butter again. Place a portion of chicken and garlic cloves that have been lightly mashed with a fork along the short end of the filo. Top with a sixteenth of the prosciutto and ½ cup cheese. Fold in the sides and roll up. Repeat with remaining filo sheets. Work quickly so filo doesn't dry out. Place rolls on lightly greased baking sheet and brush them with butter. Bake at 400 degrees F. about 20 minutes, until golden.

Makes 6 rolls.

KISS-ME-NOW CHICKEN

This recipe was a huge favorite with the judges back in '83.

Regional Winner 1983 Recipe Contest: **Emmalea Kelley, Greenbelt, MD**

2 heads fresh garlic

1 cup water

1 fryer chicken (about 3 to 4 pounds)

1/4 teaspoon *each* black pepper and dill weed

1/4 teaspoon salad oil

1/4 pound fresh mushrooms, rinsed and trimmed

6 (1-inch) pieces celery

2 tablespoons flour

1 tablespoon cooking sherry

1 cup half-and-half

Separate garlic cloves and discard loose skin, but do not peel. Boil garlic in water in a small saucepan for 30 minutes. Meanwhile, entering from the neck and rear sections of the chicken, break the membranes that attach the skin to the body with your index finger. Remove all fat from the chicken. Strain water from the garlic into a small bowl and reserve. Scatter garlic on a plate to cool. Press each clove from the pointed end into a small bowl. Discard skins. Preheat oven to 350 degrees F. Add pepper and dill to garlic paste in a bowl and blend well. Spoon half the mixture under the skin of the chicken, patting gently to distribute evenly. Spread remainder of garlic mixture inside chicken. Place chicken in a lightly oiled shallow baking dish and fill bird cavity with mushrooms. Arrange celery around chicken. Bake at 350 degrees F. for 1 1/2 hours, basting every 15 minutes with reserved garlic liquid. Remove chicken to a serving dish. Remove mushrooms and chop. Discard celery. Scrape drippings from the baking dish into a small pan. Stir flour into the pan drippings. Add mushrooms, sherry, and half-and-half. Bring to a boil, stirring constantly. Turn off heat and stir until well thickened. Quarter the chicken and serve with sauce.

Makes 4 servings.

CALIFORNIA CHICKEN

In this recipe, the beautiful presentation, which includes colorful slices of California avocado and mandarin oranges, is not just for garnish but also lends fresh flavors to a savory garlicky classic.

Finalist 1984 Recipe Contest: Jan E. Shelton, Escondido, CA

60 cloves (about 5 heads) fresh garlic

Boiling water

3 cups whipping cream

Salt and white pepper to taste

¹/₄ cup butter

4 whole chicken breasts, split, skinned, and boned

¹/₈ teaspoon *each* cinnamon and dried tarragon

2 ripe avocados

Juice of 1 lime

1 (6-ounce) can mandarin orange slices, drained

1 tablespoon chopped fresh parsley

Paprika

Place garlic cloves in a saucepan with boiling water to cover. Boil 2 minutes. Drain, and peel cloves. Return garlic to the pan and add whipping cream. Simmer, stirring occasionally, until garlic is very tender and cream is thickened and reduced by half. Rub garlic and cream through a wire sieve. Return to the saucepan and season with salt and pepper. Set aside and place plastic wrap on cream surface. Heat butter in a skillet over medium-high heat. Add chicken and sauté 1 minute, turning chicken once. Do not brown. Place chicken in an ovenproof platter. Bake in 325-degree F. oven 7 to 10 minutes. Meanwhile, peel avocados, cut into ¹/₂-inch slices, and toss with lime juice. Pour garlic mixture over chicken and return to oven for 2 or 3 minutes. Garnish with drained avocado and orange slices. Sprinkle with chopped fresh parsley and paprika to taste. Serve at once.

Makes 4 to 6 servings.

CHICKEN PEPERONATA

The combination of garlic, peppers, and balsamic vinegar makes a zesty sauce for this chicken.

Finalist 1983 Recipe Contest: **Stacey Haroldsen, Los Angeles, CA**

2 whole chickens (about 3 pounds each)

2 tablespoons butter

2 whole heads fresh garlic

Salt and pepper

2 large sprigs fresh rosemary

3 large green bell peppers

3 large red bell peppers

¼ cup pine nuts

¼ cup extra virgin olive oil

¼ cup Italian balsamic vinegar

1 tablespoon sugar

3 tablespoons chopped fresh basil

Lettuce leaves and basil sprigs for garnish

Preheat oven to 375 degrees F. Wash chickens and pat dry; rub with butter. Separate cloves of garlic, but do not peel. Sprinkle cavities of chickens with salt and pepper; place a sprig of rosemary and half of the garlic cloves in each. Roast breast-side down for 1 hour, then turn breast-side up and continue roasting until tender, about 15 minutes. Remove from oven. When cool enough to handle, remove meat from bones, pulling the meat into strips. Reserve cooked garlic cloves. Broil peppers until skins are charred, then hold under running water while removing skins and seeds. Cut half the peppers into strips and reserve the rest. Remove skins from 6 of the cooked garlic cloves and mince finely. Toast pine nuts in a dry skillet over medium heat. Combine olive oil, vinegar, and sugar in a bowl. Toss chicken, peppers, pine nuts, basil, minced garlic, and dressing. Add salt and pepper to taste. Line a serving platter with lettuce and mound chicken salad on top. Garnish with the reserved peppers, the cooked garlic cloves (skins and all), and basil sprigs. Serve at room temperature.

Makes 6 to 8 servings.

SPICY GARLIC CHICKEN

This dish is at its best when the chicken is allowed to marinate overnight in the refrigerator.

Finalist 1984 Recipe Contest: **Cindy Neva, Acton, CA**

Spicy Chicken

1 bunch cilantro, with roots

1 large whole head fresh garlic, peeled

2 tablespoons coarsely ground black pepper

1 teaspoon ground curry powder

1/4 teaspoon crushed red chile pepper

1/4 cup peanut oil

1/3 cup soy sauce

1 whole chicken *or* 12 drumsticks, wings, or thighs

Sweet Garlic Dipping Sauce (see recipe below)

Sweet Garlic Dipping Sauce

3 cups sugar

1 cup vinegar

2 tablespoons coarsely ground black pepper

1 teaspoon dry red chile pepper

1/2 teaspoon salt

1 drop red food coloring

1 whole head fresh garlic, peeled and chopped

Cut off cilantro roots and place in a food processor with garlic, some cilantro leaves, and a few stems and whirl until coarsely chopped, or chop by hand. Turn mixture into a bowl, add remaining whole cilantro leaves, pepper, curry powder, chili pepper, peanut oil, and soy sauce. Mix well. Pour mixture over chicken and marinate at least 4 hours, or overnight. Meanwhile, prepare Sweet Garlic Dipping Sauce. Barbecue chicken over low glowing coals about 1 hour, basting several times. Serve with Sweet Garlic Dipping Sauce.

To make the sweet garlic dipping sauce: In a 2-quart saucepan, bring sugar and vinegar to boil. Add pepper, chile pepper, salt, and food coloring. Boil 5 minutes, stirring to prevent sticking. (Be careful not to permit mixture to boil over pan.) Remove from heat and stir in chopped garlic. Refrigerate.

Makes 4 servings.

SHANGHAI CHICKEN ON SHANGHAI RICE

To prepare this Chinese-style chicken dish in advance, bone the chicken after it cools and combine the chicken and sauce with rice in a casserole. Reheat before serving.

Recipe Contest entry: **John J. Moon, San Francisco, CA**

Shanghai Chicken

4 tablespoons oil *or* butter

12 medium onions, sliced

Freshly ground pepper

1 tablespoon soy sauce

8 chicken thighs

¼ cup grated ginger root, or more if desired

10 cloves fresh garlic, minced, or more if desired

½ cup oyster sauce

2 tablespoons Worcestershire

Shanghai Rice

1 cup rice

½ pound ham, cut into small chunks

1 cup peas, fresh *or* frozen

Fresh ginger root (optional) peeled and cut into small chunks

Heat oil or butter in a large skillet over medium heat. Add onions and pepper and sauté until onions are golden. Stir in soy sauce. Add chicken, skin-side down with skin touching the skillet, and continue cooking. While skin browns, top chicken with equal amounts of grated ginger and minced garlic. Turn chicken over so that garlic and ginger are underneath and continue cooking, lowering heat if necessary to prevent burning. Cover chicken with onions and cook about 10 minutes more. Turn chicken again and top each thigh with oyster sauce. Cook 5 minutes more, turning chicken once. Cook 5 minutes, turn chicken, and stir Worcestershire sauce into the onions. Continue cooking until chicken is thoroughly brown and onions have reduced to form a sauce. Total cooking time is approximately 1 hour.

To make the Shanghai rice: Prepare rice according to package directions. Cook the ham, peas, and optional ginger in with the rice. Serve chicken over rice.

Makes 4 to 6 servings.

WILD RICE AND CHICKEN

Wild rice, which is not rice at all but the grain of a tall, aquatic North American grass, is a true delicacy. It is prepared like ordinary rice, but takes a little longer to cook and is well worth the extra time.

Recipe Contest entry: **M. Shipman, San Francisco, CA**

1 cup uncooked wild rice

2 ¼ cups chicken broth

8 to 10 cloves fresh garlic, minced or pressed

2 tablespoons soy sauce

2 teaspoons poultry seasoning

Coarsely ground black pepper

½ pound mushrooms, sliced

1 green bell pepper, chopped

6 stalks of celery, chopped

6 half chicken breasts, boned and skinned

Chopped green onions for garnish

Rinse rice well, at least 3 times. In a casserole, place chicken broth, garlic, soy sauce, poultry seasoning, and black pepper. Stir. Then add rice, mushrooms, bell pepper, and celery. Mix well. Bury the chicken in rice-vegetable mixture. Cover, and bake at 350 degrees F. for 1 hour. Remove from the oven, and let stand, covered, for 30 minutes. Garnish with sliced green onions and serve.

Makes 6 servings.

CHICKEN TOSCANO

This entrée can be prepared ahead in a large baking dish, covered with foil, and refrigerated. It may take slightly longer to cook if cold when placed in the oven.

Recipe Contest entry: **Carole A. Lake, Gilroy, CA**

1 fryer chicken (about 3 to 3½ pounds) cut into serving-sized pieces

Flour

Cooking oil

6 cloves fresh garlic, minced

3 medium leaves fresh basil, chopped fine

½ cup chopped fresh parsley

1 (5-ounce) can button mushrooms, drained

¼ cup butter

⅓ cup dry white wine

Salt and pepper to taste

Fresh parsley sprigs for garnish (optional)

Dredge chicken in flour and brown in oil over medium heat. Place browned chicken in a large baking dish and set aside. Sauté garlic, basil, and parsley in butter. Drizzle evenly over chicken. Slowly pour wine and mushrooms over. Salt and pepper lightly; cover with foil, and bake at 350 degrees F. for 40 minutes or until done. Garnish with parsley sprigs, if desired.

Makes 4 servings.

Garlic—from ancient times, it's imparted its potent powers.

—*Indianapolis Star*

GARLIC CHICKEN WITH PLUM SAUCE

The Pickled Garlic is an outstanding condiment but must be made at least a month before you prepare the chicken dish. Be sure to make several batches.

Recipe Contest entry: **Kathleen McElroy, Madison, WI**

Pickled Garlic

2 to 3 heads garlic

White vinegar

Sugar

Garlic Chicken

1 chicken breast, skinned, boned, and partially frozen for easy slicing

2 tablespoons Chinese plum sauce

1 tablespoon Japanese soy sauce

1 tablespoon cornstarch

1 1/2 teaspoons pickled garlic vinegar

6 to 8 large dried Chinese mushrooms

2 scallions *or* green onions

4 large cloves Pickled Garlic (see recipe above)

2 thin slices fresh ginger

5 tablespoons vegetable oil

Place garlic, unpeeled, but separated into cloves, into a small jar with a tightly fitting lid. Add white vinegar and sugar to cover, adding 1/2 teaspoon sugar for each 1/2 cup vinegar. Refrigerate 1 month before using. Keeps indefinitely.

To make the garlic chicken: Slice chicken breast thin; combine with 1 tablespoon plum sauce, soy sauce, cornstarch, and the pickled garlic vinegar. Set aside and let stand 30 minutes. Meanwhile, soak mushrooms in lukewarm water 30 minutes. Squeeze mushrooms dry, cut out tough center stem, and slice into thin strips. Split scallions lengthwise and shred into 1-inch lengths. Peel Pickled Garlic and mince. Chop ginger fine. Heat oil in a wok or heavy skillet over high heat. Stir garlic and ginger in hot oil until they begin to brown. Add marinated chicken and stir until cooked through. Remove chicken and add remaining 1 tablespoon cooking oil. Quickly stir scallions, mushrooms, and remaining 1 tablespoon plum sauce in oil until vegetables are wilted. Return chicken to mixture and stir until heated through. Serve with rice.

Makes 2 servings.

Oyster Sauce Turkey Breast with Peas and Mushrooms

Although this recipe could be made with soy sauce as a substitute for oyster sauce, the dish has a much richer flavor made with the latter. Available in the Oriental section of most supermarkets, oyster sauce is a concentrated concoction of oysters cooked in soy sauce and brine.

Recipe Contest entry: **Cecilly Jacobson, Fallon, NV**

1 boned turkey breast (about 1½ pounds)

2 tablespoons vegetable oil

4 large cloves fresh garlic, peeled and minced

1 piece fresh ginger (about 2 inches long), peeled and minced

½ cup chicken stock *or* chicken bouillon

4 tablespoons oyster sauce

1 tablespoon *each* soy sauce and sherry

1 teaspoon sugar

1 (10-ounce) package frozen green peas

1 (4-ounce) can button mushrooms, drained

2 teaspoons cornstarch mixed with 2 teaspoons water

1 green onion, chopped fine

Cut turkey into 1-inch cubes. Heat oil in a wok or skillet; add garlic and ginger and stir-fry, being careful not to burn garlic. Add turkey and stir-fry to brown slightly. Combine chicken stock, oyster sauce, soy sauce, sherry, and sugar and pour over turkey, stirring to coat turkey well. Cover, reduce heat, and simmer about 5 minutes. Stir in peas and mushrooms and stir until heated through, about 2 minutes. Stir cornstarch mixture and add to turkey. Cook, stirring, until mixture thickens slightly. Serve sprinkled with green onions.

Makes 6 servings.

WOKING GARLIC CHICKEN

We've been told the Asian flavors in this recipe make it especially appealing to kids. If you don't have a wok, use a large skillet or electric frying pan.

Recipe Contest entry: **Marlene Sasaki Jose, Los Angeles, CA**

3 large dried shiitake
   mushrooms

1 pound diced, boned chicken
   breast

1 tablespoon dry white wine

$1/4$ teaspoon each salt and
   pepper

1 ($14^1/2$-ounce) can chicken
   broth

$1/4$ cup tomato paste

2 tablespoons cornstarch

2 tablespoons brandy

Salt and pepper to taste

2 tablespoons peanut oil

1 whole head fresh garlic,
   peeled and sliced

1 large green bell pepper,
   seeded and julienned

1 small onion, chopped

1 (8-ounce) can water
   chestnuts, drained
   and coarsely chopped

Cilantro for garnish

Soak dried mushrooms in a small bowl of hot water. Set aside 20 minutes. Place chicken in a bowl with a cover, and add wine and salt and pepper. Set aside. Rinse soaking mushrooms, squeeze out excess water, cut off stems at the base and discard. Slice mushrooms very thin. Combine broth, tomato paste, cornstarch, brandy, and salt and pepper; set aside. Heat wok on medium-high. Place 2 tablespoons of oil in wok. When oil begins to smoke, lift and tilt wok slightly to coat the cooking surface. Place chicken gently into the oil and toss to stir-fry 2 minutes, or until chicken turns white and no pink shows. Remove chicken from wok. Add 1 tablespoon oil; when oil begins to smoke, add garlic, green pepper, and onion. Stir-fry 2 to 3 minutes. Add water chestnuts and mushrooms; stir-fry 1 minute. Return chicken to wok and pour sauce mixture over. Cook 5 minutes, stirring occasionally. Sauce will thicken. Serve on rice and garnish with cilantro.

Makes 4 servings.

CHINESE CHICKEN WINGS

Increase temperature to decrease baking time. Try 375 F. degrees for an hour if you need this dish in a hurry.

Recipe Contest entry: **Robyn Flipse, Ocean, NJ**

3 to 4 pounds chicken wings

Salt and pepper to taste

5 tablespoons honey

4 tablespoons soy sauce

3 tablespoons brown sugar

1 tablespoon minced fresh garlic

1 teaspoon lemon juice

6 peppercorns

1 cup hot water

Cut tips from chicken wings and reserve for another use. Cut remaining wing in half at the joint. Rinse chicken and pat dry. Place in an ungreased, shallow baking pan in a single layer. Sprinkle with salt and pepper. Mix together in a small jar the remaining ingredients; cover and shake well. Pour mixture over wings. Cover pan with foil and bake 2 hours at 325 degrees F. Remove foil, reduce heat to 300 degrees F., and continue baking another 30 minutes, basting wings with drippings every 10 minutes. When wings are brown, remove and drain on paper towels. Serve hot or cold.

Makes 4 to 5 servings.

HODGE-PODGE CHICKEN BAKE

Garlic devotees may wish to up the ante on the garlic for a more dominant flavor.

Recipe Contest entry: **Cynthia Kannenberg, Brown Deer, WI**

2 fryer chickens (about 3 ½ pounds each), each cut into 8 pieces

Salt and pepper to taste

1 tablespoon paprika

1 (1-pound 4-ounce) can pineapple chunks

1 (8-ounce) can tomato sauce

1 (6-ounce) can frozen orange juice concentrate

6 cloves fresh garlic, minced

¼ cup packed brown sugar

1 teaspoon cinnamon

½ teaspoon dry mustard

1 (11-ounce) can mandarin orange segments, drained

Sprinkle chicken on all sides with salt, pepper, and paprika. Place in a large 12 x 18-inch roasting pan. Drain pineapple, reserving juice. Mix 1 cup pineapple juice with tomato sauce, orange juice concentrate, garlic, sugar, cinnamon, and mustard; pour over chicken. Bake at 350 degrees F. about 1¼ hours, basting every 15 minutes. Add more pineapple juice, if necessary. Add pineapple chunks during the final 5 minutes of baking. Serve on a bed of hot rice; garnish with orange segments.

Makes 8 servings.

CHICKEN CURRY WITH PEACHES

Definitely a dish for company that takes a little time to prepare but is truly worth the effort.

Recipe Contest entry: **Karen Harmatulk, San Francisco, CA**

½ cup butter

½ cup chopped onion

4 cloves fresh garlic, minced *or* pressed

2 teaspoons curry powder

3 teaspoons paprika

6 chicken half breasts *or* thighs

1 bunch broccoli, cut into pieces

1 small head cauliflower, separated into flowerets

¾ cup dry white wine

12 canned *or* fresh peach halves, sliced

2 cups yogurt

½ cup mayonnaise

½ cup grated Monterey Jack cheese

Melt butter in a small skillet. Add onion and garlic; sauté until onion is soft. Stir in curry and paprika. Dredge chicken in mixture, coating well. Place chicken in a shallow baking dish. Steam broccoli and cauliflower briefly and arrange among chicken pieces. Carefully drizzle wine between chicken pieces. Cover loosely with foil and bake 30 minutes at 375 degrees F. Remove from oven and discard foil. Place peaches among chicken and vegetables. Mix yogurt and mayonnaise and spoon over chicken. Sprinkle with cheese. Place on the lower oven rack and broil 8 to 10 minutes, or until lightly browned.

Makes 6 servings.

PHONY ABALONE

The longer the chicken marinates, the more it tastes like abalone. And you can change the recipe to "Unreal Veal" by adding Parmesan cheese to the breadcrumbs and omitting the tartar sauce.

Recipe Contest entry: **Sylvia Walker, Monterey, CA**

4 chicken breast halves, boned, skinned, and sliced into thin steaks

1 (8-ounce) bottle clam juice

6 cloves fresh garlic, peeled and halved

2 eggs, lightly beaten

1 1/2 cups fine breadcrumbs

4 to 6 tablespoons butter

Lemon wedges

Tartar sauce (optional)

Place chicken steaks between two sheets of waxed paper and pound thin. Place in a flat, airtight container. Pour clam juice over and add fresh garlic. Cover, and refrigerate 36 to 48 hours, turning chicken once or twice if clam juice does not cover completely. Drain chicken. Dip in beaten egg, then dredge in breadcrumbs. Sauté lightly in butter. Serve with lemon wedges and tartar sauce, if desired.

Makes 4 servings.

If you face toward Gilroy and take a deep breath, you can almost smell the good times being cooked up for the weekend.

—*San Jose Mercury News*

CHICKEN KARMA

Lovers of Indian cuisine as well as garlic will love this dish. Some may wish to cut back a bit on the ginger.

Recipe Contest entry: **Elizabeth Balderston, Ramona, CA**

4 tablespoons butter

I large onion, thinly sliced

6 cloves fresh garlic, sliced

I tablespoon fresh ginger, diced

³/₄ teaspoon whole cumin seed

¹/₂ teaspoon *each* coriander and mustard seed

¹/₂ teaspoon crush red chiles

3 chicken breasts, skinned, boned, and cubed

3 tablespoons raw almonds, ground (in a blender or food processor)

I teaspoon turmeric

¹/₂ teaspoon salt

¹/₄ teaspoon *each* ground cloves and cinnamon

¹/₂ cup plain yogurt

¹/₄ cup chopped fresh cilantro

I tablespoon lemon juice

Melt butter in a large, heavy skillet or Dutch oven over medium-high heat. Cook onion, garlic, and ginger until onion is tender. Add cumin, coriander seed, mustard seed, and chiles; cook 2 minutes. Add chicken; stir and cook until chicken begins to turn white. Stir in almonds, turmeric, salt, cloves, and cinnamon; cook 1 minute more. Add yogurt; stir until blended, then reduce heat, cover and simmer 1 hour. Just before serving, stir in cilantro and lemon juice. Serve over rice.

Makes 4 servings.

THIRTY-CLOVE CHICKEN

Not only will this dish banish evil spirits, but it will raise good ones, we're told, especially those of garlic loves, for it contains 30 whole cloves!

Recipe Contest entry: **Leah Jackson, Marshfield, MA**

2 fryer chickens, cut into serving-sized pieces

4 tablespoons olive oil

2 tablespoons butter

1 tablespoons flour

1 (14 1/2-ounce) can chicken broth

30 cloves fresh garlic, peeled

1 cup rice

Fresh chives and parsley, minced

Brown the chicken in 2 tablespoons oil and butter. Remove from pan and stir in flour; then add broth and garlic. Bring to a boil, return chicken to pan and simmer, covered, 45 minutes. Sauté rice in remaining 2 tablespoons of oil until rice is opaque. Add rice to chicken, gently stirring into liquid with a fork. Cover, and simmer another 25 minutes. Just before serving, stir in fresh herbs.

Makes 8 servings.

GYPSY GARLIC CHICKEN

The garlic lover's adaptation of a classic recipe that always begins: "First you steal the chicken…"

Recipe Contest entry: **Jeanne D'Avray, Metairie, LA**

21 or more cloves fresh garlic, peeled

8 chicken breast halves *plus* 4 legs

2 tablespoons cooking oil

2 medium onions, sliced

1 1/2 cups water

1 (8-ounce) can tomato sauce

1/2 cup dry sherry

2 tablespoons sugar

1 tablespoon vinegar

1 teaspoon *each* salt and chervil

2 large bay leaves

1 heaping teaspoon whole peppercorns

1 cheesecloth square (about 4 x 4 inches)

Lemon slices and parsley for garnish

Cut 5 garlic cloves into thin slices. Using a sharp knife, pierce chicken skin at 1 1/2-inch intervals and insert garlic slices between the skin and meat. Heat oil to medium-high and sauté chicken, onions, and remaining whole garlic cloves until chicken is slightly browned, stirring often so onions and garlic do not burn. Add water, tomato sauce, sherry, sugar, vinegar, salt, and chervil; bring to a boil. Wrap bay leaves and peppercorns in cheesecloth and tie opposite ends to make a bag. Drop into boiling sauce; reduce heat, cover, and simmer 25 to 30 minutes until chicken is tender. Remove spice bag. Secure a parsley sprig into center of 8 lemon slices with a toothpick. Place atop larger pieces of meat, cover, and simmer 8 minutes. Arrange on a platter, garnished with additional fresh parsley, if desired. Serve at once, with buttered egg noodles.

Makes 8 servings.

CHICKEN AND SAUSAGE RAGOUT ALLA ROSINA

The definition of "ragout" is a "highly seasoned dish of stewed meat and vegetables." In this recipe, the seasoning begins with 20 cloves of fresh garlic, the meat includes chicken and spicy Italian sausage, and the vegetables are mushrooms and red peppers—and the finished product is outstanding. And it's even better the next day.

Recipe Contest entry: **Rosina Wilson, Albany, CA**

1 fryer chicken (about 3 pounds), cut into small pieces

1 pound Italian-style fennel sausages, halved

¼ cup olive oil

1 large onion, minced

½ pound button mushrooms

20 or more cloves fresh garlic, peeled

⅓ cup brandy

1 (28-ounce) can Italian-style plum tomatoes, chopped

2 cups red wine

3 bay leaves

½ teaspoon fennel seeds

1 roasted red pepper, cut into strips

3 sprigs *each* fresh oregano and parsley

12 ounces fusilli

Parmesan cheese, freshly grated

In a large skillet, brown the chicken and sausages in oil. Transfer to a large heatproof casserole. Sauté onion, mushrooms, and garlic briefly in oil that remains; add brandy, then increase heat and ignite. Pour mixture along with tomatoes, wine, bay leaves, and fennel seeds into the casserole and simmer 1 hour, skimming fat frequently. Add roasted pepper, oregano, and parsley; simmer 10 minutes more to blend flavors. Skim fat, add salt and pepper. Serve over fusilli pasta that has been cooked *al dente* according to package directions. Sprinkle liberally with Parmesan cheese.

Makes 4 to 6 servings.

CHICKEN MAUI

Pineapple slices, lichee nuts, and kumquats add a touch of the Hawaiian Islands to this recipe.

Recipe Contest entry: **Barbara Cohen, Philadelphia, PA**

1 pound ground pork

1 small onion, minced

3 or more cloves fresh garlic, minced

2 scallions *or* green onions, chopped

2 tablespoons oil

½ cup breadcrumbs

1 egg

¼ cup *plus* 1 tablespoon soy sauce

1 (8-ounce) can water chestnuts, drained and chopped

6 small whole chicken breasts, boned and skinned

½ cup chicken broth

1 tablespoon honey

Black pepper to taste

6 tablespoons sesame seeds

1 large (15¼-ounce) can pineapple slices, drained

1 (11-ounce) can lichee nuts, drained

1 (8-ounce) jar kumquats, drained

Curly parsley

In a large skillet, sauté pork, onion, garlic, and scallions in oil until pork loses pinkness. Remove from heat. Add breadcrumbs, egg, ¼ cup soy sauce, and water chestnuts. Stuff chicken breasts with this mixture, and secure with toothpicks or wooden skewers. In a large baking dish, mix honey, 1 tablespoon soy sauce, and pepper. Place chicken in baking pan and bake 35 minutes at 325 degrees F., turning once and basting. Sprinkle with sesame seeds and top with pineapple. Broil 3 minutes and remove to a heated platter. Garnish with lichee nuts, kumquats, and curly parsley.

Makes 6 servings.

HERBED CHEESE AND CHICKEN IN PUFF PASTRY

A lovely main course for family and guests that makes a beautiful presentation but is deceptively easy to prepare.

Recipe Contest entry: **Mary Jane Himel, Palo Alto, CA**

20 large cloves fresh garlic

6 chicken thighs

2 1/2 cups chicken broth

9 slices bacon, fried

5 ounces cream cheese

1 1/2 teaspoons tarragon

1 (10-ounce) package frozen puff pastry patty shells, thawed

1 egg, slightly beaten

Blanch garlic in boiling water 1 minute. Peel garlic and place with chicken and broth in a saucepan. Simmer gently, covered, 30 minutes. Remove chicken and garlic from both. Skin chicken and remove bones. Place 1 1/2 slices of bacon where the bones were. Purée garlic with 3 tablespoons broth, cream cheese, and tarragon. On lightly floured board, roll out a pastry shell into an 8-inch circle. Place a stuffed chicken thigh on top, then 2 tablespoons garlic-cheese mixture. Moisten the edges of the pastry with your finger dipped in cold water. Gather edges at the top and crimp to seal. Repeat with remaining 5 shells. Place filled pastries on a lightly buttered baking sheet. Brush tops with beaten egg and bake at 400 degrees F. for 25 minutes, or until golden brown.

Makes 6 servings.

Garlic is a cook's best friend.

—*Chicago Sun-Times*

SQUABS SANTA CRUZ

Squab is a term used in the U.S. and Britain for a young pigeon, weighing usually no more than a pound. If not available, substitute Rock Cornish game hens.

Recipe Contest entry: **Lisa Gorman, San Francisco, CA**

2 squabs (about 1 to
1 1/4 pounds each)

6 tablespoons butter

8 cloves fresh garlic, peeled
and finely chopped

1 medium tomato, peeled,
seeded, and finely chopped

2 tablespoons chopped parsley

Pinch thyme

1/2 cup dry white wine

Garlic salt and pepper to taste

Lemon pepper and salt to taste
(optional)

6 fresh mushrooms, sliced

Split squabs and remove breast bones. In a skillet, sear squabs on both sides in hot butter. Add garlic, tomato, parsley, and thyme. Blend well, then add wine, salt, and pepper. Cover and cook over low heat, about 30 minutes. Add mushrooms and continue cooking 10 to 15 minutes until squab is tender. Serve garnished with thin slices of orange with noodles or rice.

Makes 2 to 3 servings.

SEAFOOD

GRILLED FISH WITH GARLIC SALSA

"To win first prize, improvise," said Beverly Stone, and improvise she did. Her recipe was developed out of necessity when she found herself with only a few ingredients which, when combined, became an outstanding new garlic salsa to serve over fish. The judges agreed it was quite a catch.

Winner 1984 Recipe Contest: **Beverly Stone, Berkeley, CA**

Fish

¹/₂ cup olive oil

5 tablespoons lemon juice

4 cloves fresh garlic, peeled and slivered

I bunch fresh cilantro, chopped to make ¹/₂ cup, reserving some whole leaves for garnish

Salt and freshly ground pepper to taste

6 firm-fleshed fish fillets (about 6 ounces each, about ³/₄-inch thick)

Garlic Salsa

¹/₄ pound sweet butter

¹/₄ cup chopped sweet red onion

2 small hot green chiles, finely minced

I tablespoon finely minced fresh garlic

I pound ripe tomatoes, peeled and chopped

Lemon wedges

Combine olive oil, 4 tablespoons lemon juice, slivered garlic, ¹/₄ cup chopped cilantro, and salt and pepper to taste. Add fish fillets and marinate 1 hour or overnight. Meanwhile, prepare Garlic Salsa. Barbecue fish over low glowing coals, about 7 minutes, or until done to your liking, turning fish once. Remove to a warm serving platter. Top with Garlic Salsa. Garnish with lemon wedges and reserved cilantro leaves.

To make the garlic salsa: In a frying pan over medium heat, melt 2 tablespoons butter. Sauté onion, chiles, and minced garlic until soft, stirring continuously. Add tomatoes and the remaining 1 tablespoon lemon juice. Cook 10 minutes, stirring continuously. Remove from heat, and add salt and pepper to taste. Stir in remaining ¹/₃ cup chopped cilantro. Slowly stir in remaining butter until melted.

Makes 6 servings.

JAMBALAYA CREOLE

To make Jambalaya "Santa Cruz-style," just substitute calamari for the shrimp. Serve with hot corn-bread or sweet French bread.

Recipe Contest entry: **Bruce Engelhardt, Santa Cruz, CA**

1 1/2 pounds cooked shrimp

1 pound smoked rope-style
    sausage, cut into 1/4-inch
    slices

1 pound ham, diced

1/2 cup cooking oil

1/2 cup flour

1 red onion, finely chopped

1 cup chopped green bell pepper

2 stalks celery, finely chopped

2 shallots, chopped

4 or more cloves fresh garlic,
    chopped

2 tomatoes, chopped

1 (16-ounce) can tomato sauce

1 tablespoon crushed oregano

1 teaspoon salt

1/2 teaspoon chopped fresh
    cilantro

1/4 teaspoon *each* red pepper,
    black pepper, ground cloves,
    allspice, and cumin

1 cup red wine

2 bay leaves

1/2 cup chopped parsley

1 cup hot water

2 cups long grain white rice

1/4 cup chopped green onion
    tops for garnish

Louisiana-style hot sauce,
    if desired

Clean shrimp and set aside. Brown sausage and ham in oil; set aside. Stir in flour and cook, stirring frequently, until dark brown in color and syrupy. Add more oil or more flour, if necessary. Add one at a time the onion, celery, bell pepper, shallots, and garlic, cooking each until just done before adding the next. Add tomatoes, stirring to prevent sticking. Stir in tomato sauce, then oregano, salt, cilantro, and spices, wine, and bay leaves. Simmer sauce 20 minutes until flavors are well blended. Add more wine if sauce becomes too thick. Add parsley, sausage, ham, and water and raise heat to a high simmer. Add rice and shrimp and reduce heat to low, cover, and cook about 20 minutes, or until rice is done. Garnish with green onions and serve with Louisiana-style hot sauce for extra zest.

Makes 12 servings.

SUPERSONIC FISH STEW

Some might call this stew, others insist it's chowder. No matter what you call it, we think you'll love it.

Recipe Contest entry: **Jacqueline McComas, Frazer, PA**

2 tablespoons cooking oil

1 cup chopped onions

3 cloves fresh garlic, minced

1/4 cup *each* chopped green bell pepper and celery

2 pounds assorted seafood, cut up (scallops, shrimp, flounder, etc., or a combination)

1 (10 3/4-ounce) can condensed tomato soup, undiluted

1 (10 3/4-ounce) can condensed clam chowder, undiluted

1 soup can water

1/4 cup dry white wine

4 tablespoons minced parsley

Salt and pepper to taste

2 tablespoons minced chives for garnish

In a large saucepan, heat oil; add onions, garlic, bell pepper, and celery. Sauté until vegetables are lightly cooked. Add fish, soups, water, wine, 2 tablespoons parsley, and salt and pepper. Bring to a boil and simmer 20 minutes, or until fish is done. Sprinkle with remaining parsley and/or chives and serve with plenty of crusty bread.

Makes 6 to 8 servings.

GARLIC CLAMS

Lots of hot sourdough French bread is a must to sop up the delicious juices!

Recipe Contest entry: **Roberta Robinson, Campbell, CA**

12 cloves fresh garlic, minced

1 bunch green onions, minced

½ cup butter

¼ cup vegetable oil

½ cup chopped parsley

1 teaspoon Italian seasoning

1 cup *each* dry white wine,
    clam juice, and water

24 cherrystone clams, brushed
    and cleaned

In a large skillet, sauté garlic and onions in butter and oil for 1 minute. Add parsley and seasoning. Add wine, clam juice, and water and cook 2 minutes. Now add clams and cook, covered, until clams open, about 10 to 12 minutes. Serve in bowls.

Makes 2 servings.

MARINATED SQUID ALLA ROSINA

An outstanding recipe from the winner of the 1982 Recipe Contest. For best flavor, be sure to prepare this several hours before serving time.

Recipe Contest entry: **Rosina Wilson, Albany, CA**

3 pounds squid

¼ cup olive oil

⅛ cup *each* lemon juice and red wine vinegar

1 tablespoon Dijon-style mustard

Salt and pepper to taste

1 medium purple onion, coarsely chopped

1 roasted red bell pepper, cut in strips

½ cup baby carrots, sliced diagonally and lightly poached

½ cup Niçoise olives

¼ cup chopped parsley

6 cloves fresh garlic, sliced

3 tablespoons capers

1 tablespoon slivered lemon peel

Lettuce for garnish

Clean squid and cut into rings. Poach in boiling water in small batches for 30 seconds. Drain well. Prepare marinade by mixing olive oil, lemon juice, vinegar, mustard, and salt and pepper. Set aside. Combine squid and remaining ingredients in a large bowl and pour marinade over. Refrigerate several hours. Serve over lettuce or as an appetizer salad.

Makes 8 servings.

BAKED SQUID SICILIANO

This recipe can be prepared ahead of time, refrigerated, and baked just before serving.

Recipe Contest entry: **Kay Lucido, Hollister, CA**

2 pounds squid, cleaned and drained

¹/₄ cup vegetable oil

1 bunch parsley, chopped

1 cup toasted breadcrumbs

¹/₂ cup *each* grated Parmesan and Romano cheese

3 cloves fresh garlic, minced

1 teaspoon oregano

Salt and pepper to taste

Dip squid in oil. Combine remaining ingredients. Roll oiled squid in breadcrumb mixture; roll up and place on an oiled jelly-roll pan, cut-side down. Bake in a preheated 425-degree F. oven for 20 minutes.

Makes 4 servings.

CALAMARI MEDITERRANEAN

An outstanding dish, best served over fresh fettuccine or linguine with freshly grated Romano cheese.

Recipe Contest entry: **Karen Occhipinti, Los Gatos, CA**

4 pounds calamari, cleaned

I cup *plus* 3 tablespoons butter

¹/₂ cup olive oil

10 cloves fresh garlic, minced

Salt and pepper to taste

¹/₃ cup dry white wine

I pound small to medium
    fresh mushrooms, cut
    into quarters

3 medium ripe tomatoes,
    peeled and chopped

¹/₂ cup chopped fresh parsley

4 to 5 tablespoons fresh
    chopped basil *or*
    I teaspoon dried basil

Cut calamari into wide strips and rings. Melt 3 table-spoons of butter in a large skillet. Add 3 tablespoons oil, half the garlic, calamari, salt, and pepper and sauté 2 minutes. Do not overcook. Drain and reserve liquid. Set calamari aside. In the same skillet, melt 1 cup butter, then add remaining oil, all but 1 tablespoon of garlic, and wine: simmer 1 to 2 minutes. Add mushrooms, tomatoes, and ¼ cup parsley. Simmer over low heat 8 to 10 minutes. Add basil and remaining garlic. For thinner consistency, if desired, add reserved liquid. Simmer 2 minutes longer. Serve sprinkled with remaining parsley.

Makes 8 servings.

Garlic revered as food, folk
remedy for millennia.

—Topeka Daily Capital

SQUID GILROY FOR TWO

Serve this squid dish alone or over spaghetti with a light, fruity Zinfandel and fresh vegetables.

Recipe Contest entry: **Dr. E. Stoddard, Monterey, CA**

2 pounds squid, cleaned and drained

3 to 4 green onions, sliced

3 large cloves fresh garlic, sliced

4 teaspoons olive oil

1 (8-ounce) can tomato sauce

½ cup red wine

½ cup chopped parsley

3 teaspoons Italian seasoning

½ cup grated Parmesan cheese

Cut squid into rings. In a large skillet, cook onions and garlic in oil until lightly brown, about 2 minutes. Add squid when pan is hot and cook about 10 minutes, stirring occasionally. Add tomato sauce, wine, parsley, and seasoning. Simmer 10 minutes. Sprinkle with Parmesan, stir well, and leave for 1 minute to blend flavors before serving.

Makes 2 servings.

DUNGENESS CRAB DIJONNAISE

Dungeness crab usually weigh about three pounds, are native to the Pacific Northwest, and have a distinctively sweet taste. Any crabmeat can be substituted if Dungeness is not available. Best served over pasta such as fettuccine.

Recipe Contest entry: **Norman Noakes, Corvallis, OR**

1 pound Dungeness crabmeat

4 tablespoons butter

3 cloves fresh garlic, minced

1/2 pound fresh mushrooms, thinly sliced

2 tablespoons finely chopped shallots *or* scallions *or* green onions

1/2 cup dry white wine

1/2 cup whipping cream

1 tablespoon Dijon-style mustard

Salt and pepper to taste

Lemon juice to taste

Minced fresh parsley

In a skillet, sauté crab in butter for 3 to 4 minutes. Remove crab and keep warm. Add garlic, shallots, and mushrooms. Cook 1 minute. Deglaze pan with wine. Reduce to 2 tablespoons. Add cream and reduce until thick. Whisk in mustard. Do not boil. Add salt, pepper, and lemon juice. Return crab to pan and toss quickly in sauce. Serve over pasta. Sprinkle with parsley.

Makes 4 servings.

TROUT SAUTÉ ALLA ROSINA

Contest winner Rosina Wilson definitely has a way with garlic, and her recipes are always relatively easy to prepare, something other busy people will appreciate.

Recipe Contest entry: **Rosina Wilson, Albany, CA**

4 trout (about 12 ounces each)

¹/₄ cup olive oil

¹/₂ cup *each* fine cornmeal and freshly grated Parmesan cheese

¹/₄ teaspoon salt

¹/₄ cup butter

20 cloves fresh garlic, minced

³/₄ cup dry white wine

¹/₄ cup minced parsley

4 tablespoons capers, including juice

Juice of 2 lemons

4 lemon wedges

Remove heads, tails, and scales from the trout. Rinse well; pat dry, then rub skin with a little of the oil. Combine cornmeal, cheese, and salt in a long bowl or dish and coat trout generously with the mixture. In a large skillet, sauté trout in butter and oil over medium heat, 5 minutes on each side. Add garlic to fish and stir in oil for 2 to 3 minutes. Add wine, parsley, capers, and lemon juice and cook 5 to 10 minutes more, turning once, until trout flakes when tested with fork. Spoon reduced wine sauce over the trout and serve with lemon wedges.

Makes 4 servings.

ALLA TAMEN FILLET OF SOLE ROLL-UPS

Flavors of the Far East take this recipe from familiar fish to exotic dish.

Recipe Contest entry: **Stella Wolf, Culver City, CA**

1 pound fillet of sole

¼ cup peanuts

6 cloves fresh garlic, peeled

4 slices fresh ginger root (about ¼-inch thick), peeled

1 tablespoon salad oil

1 tablespoon lemon juice

4 teaspoons sesame oil

1 (10-ounce) package frozen peas

1 cup sliced fresh mushrooms (optional)

1 tablespoon *each* soy sauce and lemon juice

1 teaspoon dry mustard powder

2 tablespoons sesame seeds

Rinse sole with cold water and set aside. In a blender or food processor, combine peanuts, garlic, ginger, salad oil, lemon juice, and 1 teaspoon sesame oil. Spread a quarter of the paste onto each fillet and roll up. Arrange fish rolls in 7 x 12 x 2-inch glass baking dish, surrounded by peas and mushrooms. Blend together remaining sesame oil, soy sauce, lemon juice, and mustard. Pour over fish, allowing excess to dribble down to the bottom of the baking dish. Sprinkle sesame seeds over. Cover with aluminum foil. Bake at 350 degrees F. for 15 to 20 minutes, or until fish tests done. Serve at once.

Makes 4 servings.

GARLIC SHRIMP

A very low-calorie dish which is easy to prepare and can be enjoyed by the whole family, not just the dieters.

Recipe Contest entry: Gloria Park, Los Gatos, CA

2 pounds raw shrimp (about 24 pieces)

6 cloves fresh garlic, chopped

6 scallions *or* green onions, minced

$^1/_3$ cup chopped fresh parsley

2 teaspoons dry vermouth

$^1/_2$ teaspoon soy sauce

$^1/_4$ teaspoon Tabasco

8 fresh mushrooms, sliced

Rinse shrimp; remove the legs, leaving the tails and shell intact. With a sharp knife, cut through shells down the back, leaving the shells on. De-vein the shrimp. Combine garlic, onion, parsley, vermouth, soy sauce, and Tabasco and toss with the shrimp. Marinate in the refrigerator about 1 hour. Add mushrooms and toss again. Cut 2 sheets of heavy-duty foil 18 x 36 inches. Double each sheet by folding to 18 x 18 inches. Divide shrimp mixture evenly between the 2 foil sheets, making single layers. Enclose shrimp with double folds on the tops and on both sides of the packages so that none of the juices can escape. Place each foil package on a cookie sheet and bake at 400 degrees F. for 15 to 20 minutes, until shrimp have turned pink. Serve immediately.

Makes 6 servings.

ROGER'S SCAMPI

This dish is equally delicious served over pasta or rice and can easily be increased to serve six.

Recipe Contest entry: **Roger Kirsch, San Jose, CA**

I pound large prawns (12 to 16 per pound)

4 tablespoons sweet butter

¼ cup olive oil

5 cloves fresh garlic, minced

⅛ teaspoon *each* sweet basil and oregano

Juice of 1 lemon

Salt and pepper to taste

¼ cup Triple Sec *or* Cointreau

Shell and de-vein prawns; rinse and drain. Melt butter in a medium skillet; add olive oil, garlic, basil and oregano, and lemon juice. Sauté 1 minute. Add prawns and cook until pink. Add salt and pepper and Triple Sec; cook on high heat until liquid is reduced by three-quarters. Serve over pasta or rice.

Makes 2 to 3 servings.

Garlic Shrimp au Gratin

This dish is simplicity itself, requiring only a few ingredients and a few minutes of preparation time.

Recipe courtesy of the **Fresh Garlic Association**

2 pounds raw shrimp

1 ½ sticks butter (¾ cup)

2 cups fine dry breadcrumbs

½ cup finely chopped parsley

4 cloves fresh garlic, minced *or* pressed

Salt and pepper to taste

1 cup dry sherry

Shell and de-vein shrimp. Toss into boiling water, return to a boil, and cook about 2 minutes until shrimp turn all pink. Drain. In a large skillet, melt 1 stick (½ cup) butter over low heat. Add breadcrumbs, parsley, garlic, and salt and pepper. Stir a few minutes over low heat; pour in sherry, and cook 1 minute more. Plate alternate layers of shrimp and breadcrumbs in well-buttered gratin dish, ending with breadcrumbs. Dot with remaining butter. Bake at 350 degrees F. for 10 to 15 minutes.

Makes 4 servings.

GARLIC SCALLOP SAUTÉ

Simplicity, elegance, and rich flavor—the perfect combination.

Recipe Contest entry: **Anne McDonald, Morgan Hill, CA**

1 pound scallops

³/₄ cup milk or enough to cover

¹/₃ cup flour

4 tablespoons *each* butter and cooking oil

4 cloves fresh garlic, minced

10 fresh mushrooms, thinly sliced

2 shallots, chopped (about 3 tablespoons)

1 teaspoon lemon juice

Sherry

Wash scallops thoroughly to remove sand. Place in a small bowl and add milk to cover scallops. Let stand 10 minutes. Drain well; coat with flour. Shake off excess flour and set aside. Melt butter in a large skillet, add oil and half the garlic, and cook a few seconds. Add mushrooms, shallots, and remaining garlic. Stir constantly until done. Add scallops and lemon juice; cook 2 to 3 minutes, stirring occasionally, until scallops are just done. Remove scallops to a serving platter and keep warm. Add a dash of sherry and deglaze the pan. Pour over scallops and serve.

Makes 4 servings.

SCALLOPS IN GARLIC MUSHROOM SAUCE

When preparing scallops, it is extremely important not to overcook them as they can become quite tough and chewy. They are best when cooked until just barely done or even slightly undercooked.

Recipe courtesy of the **Fresh Garlic Association**

I pound scallops

I tablespoon vegetable oil

4 cloves fresh garlic, minced

I (5-ounces) can water chestnuts, drained and sliced

I tablespoon cornstarch mixed with 2 tablespoons water

I teaspoon salt

$^1/_8$ teaspoon white pepper

I cup sliced fresh mushrooms

$^1/_3$ cup sliced green onions, including stems

Place scallops in 2 quarts lightly salted water. Bring to a boil. Drain immediately. Heat vegetable oil in a wok or skillet. Add garlic and stir-fry until golden. Add water chestnuts, soy, cornstarch mixture, salt, and pepper and mix. Add scallops and mushrooms and cook, stirring gently, until sauce thickens and coats scallops. Remove to a platter. Sprinkle with sliced green onion.

Makes 2 to 3 servings.

HELEN'S SEAFOOD TREAT

Fresh shrimp and crabmeat are baked in individual casseroles with a rich and buttery garlic sauce.

Recipe Contest entry: **Helen Cairns, Marblehead, MA**

1 ½ pounds fresh shrimp

8 cups water

3 cloves fresh garlic, chopped

1 onion, quartered

1 bay leaf

8 tablespoons butter

1 teaspoon lemon juice

¾ cup cracker crumbs

½ pound fresh crabmeat *or* lobster, scallops, or other seafood

Lemon wedges and fresh parsley for garnish

Clean shrimp. Boil in water with 1 clove garlic, onion, and bay leaf for 5 minutes. Drain. Melt butter in a skillet; add remaining garlic and lemon juice. Add half the garlic butter to cracker crumbs. Mix well and set aside. Place shrimp and crabmeat in 4 individual casseroles. Pour remaining garlic butter evenly over seafood. Sprinkle with cracker crumbs and bake at 400 degrees F. for 5 minutes. Garnish with lemon wedges and parsley; serve piping hot.

Makes 4 servings.

The most popular attraction is Gourmet Alley, a crescent of food booths backed up against a wall of wind-breaking poplars behind the hacienda. Here one finds a fast-working, sweat-dappled crew running a foundry-like outdoor kitchen of homemade barbecue grills and primitive gas-fired stoves. The fare they were turning out, however, had all the style, appearance, texture, flavor and appeal of continental cuisine patiently prepared in the stainless-steel kitchen of a gourmet restaurant.

—Sacramento Bee

SCAMPI IN BUTTER SAUCE

A Festival favorite, Val Filice has served this exceptional dish to the delight of friends and family for years. Scampi, by the way, are closely related to shrimp but have no equivalent species outside Italian waters. Substitute prawns or shrimp of medium to large size.

Recipe courtesy of **Val Filice, Gilroy, CA**

Butter Sauce

1/2 to 1 cup butter

1 tablespoon finely minced
    fresh garlic

8 ounces clam juice

1/4 cup flour

1 tablespoon minced parsley

1/3 cup white wine

Juice of 1/2 lemon

1 teaspoon dried basil

1/4 teaspoon nutmeg

Salt and pepper to taste

1/2 cup half-and-half

Scampi

2 tablespoons butter

1/3 cup olive oil

1 tablespoon minced fresh garlic

Juice of 1 lemon

1 tablespoon fresh chopped
    parsley *or* 1 teaspoon dry

1/2 teaspoon crushed red pepper

1 tablespoon fresh basil *or*
    1 teaspoon dry

1/4 cup white wine

Dash dry vermouth

Salt and pepper to taste

3 pounds scampi *or* prawns,
    de-veined and cleaned

Melt butter with garlic in a small saucepan over medium heat; do not let butter brown. In a separate bowl, mix clam juice, flour, and parsley, blending until mixture is smooth. Pour flour mixture into garlic butter, stir until smooth and well blended. Stir in wine, lemon juice, herbs, and spices, stirring constantly. Gradually add half-and-half and stir until thickened. Simmer 30 to 45 minutes.

To make the scampi: Melt butter in a large saucepan on high heat and add oil. Combine remaining ingredients, keeping scampi aside until the last minute. Add scampi and sauté until firm and slightly pink. Do not over-cook. Pour 1 cup of scampi butter over scampi. Refrigerate the rest for later use.

Makes 10 servings.

Calamari, Festival-style

One of Gourmet Alley's biggest attractions is watching the preparation of calamari. Some argue that eating it is even better. Here is Head Chef Val Filice's recipe just as it is served at the Festival.

Recipe courtesy of **Val Filice, Gilroy, CA**

Calamari

3 pounds calamari, cleaned and cut

⅓ cup olive oil

¼ cup white sherry

1 tablespoon crushed fresh garlic

½ lemon

1 teaspoon dry basil *or* 1 tablespoon fresh

1 teaspoon dry oregano *or* 1 tablespoon fresh

¼ teaspoon dry crushed red pepper

Red Sauce (see recipe below)

Red Sauce

1 pound whole, peeled tomatoes, canned *or* fresh

1 tablespoon olive oil

½ green pepper, chopped

1 stalk celery, chopped

1 medium-sized yellow onion, chopped

3 cloves fresh garlic, minced

In a large skillet, heat olive oil at high heat. Add wine and sherry and sauté crushed garlic. Squeeze the juice of ½ lemon into the skillet. Add the lemon rind; sprinkle herbs over and add calamari. Sauté calamari about 4 minutes on high heat. Do not overcook.

To make the red sauce: Mash tomatoes with potato masher and set aside. In medium-sized saucepan, heat oil, add chopped ingredients, and sauté until onion is transparent. Add mashed tomatoes and simmer 30 minutes. Pour red sauce over calamari and heat 1 minute.

Makes 10 servings.

Last, But Not Least:
A Few Miscellaneous Recipes

BUTTERS

BASIC GARLIC BUTTER
Cream ½ cup butter. Add 2 to 3 cloves fresh garlic, finely minced *or* pressed, and beat until fluffy.

GARLIC HERB BUTTERS
Add freshly chopped chives, shallots, *or* parsley to basic garlic butter.

GARLIC CHEESE BUTTERS
Add shredded *or* grated cheese of your choice to basic garlic butter.

QUICKIE GARLIC BUTTER
Use ¾ teaspoon garlic powder instead of fresh garlic. Add ¼ teaspoon salt and a dash black pepper. Let stand for 30 minutes for flavors to blend.

EASY MELT GARLIC BUTTER
Instead of creaming basic garlic butter, just heat butter and garlic in a small saucepan over low heat until butter melts. Do not brown!

EXTRA GARLICKY BUTTER
Mash 6 cloves fresh garlic into ½ cup butter.

DELICATE GARLIC BUTTER
Blanch and drain 4 cloves of fresh garlic and pound together; combine with ½ cup fresh butter. Pass the mixture through a fine sieve.

PARTY TIME GARLIC BUTTER
Moisten 1 teaspoon of instant granulated garlic with an equal amount of water. Place in a mixer bowl with 1 pound softened butter. Beat until very creamy. Let stand about 20 minutes to blend flavors. Butter may also be melted over hot water or in a food warmer and spread with a pastry brush.

Makes enough garlic butter for 100 medium-sized pieces of French or Italian bread or 200 slices of sandwich bread.

Savory Italian Seasoning Salt

Italians are lavish users of garlic in their cooking. Mrs. Romano developed this recipe not only for her own use, but she also gives it to friends and relatives who are creative cooks.

Regional Winner 1981 Recipe Contest: **Mrs. Domeni Romano, Fresno, CA**

4 whole dried red chile peppers

¹/₄ cup dehydrated minced garlic

¹/₂ cup dehydrated minced onion

¹/₄ cup dried oregano leaves

¹/₄ cup dried basil leaves

¹/₄ cup dried parsley leaves

¹/₄ cup salt

2 tablespoons dried rosemary (optional)

In a blender, at low speed, add ingredients in the order listed. Cover, and turn to high speed to pulverize and blend well. Store in a shaker with a tight lid. Use for seasoning steaks, roasts, vegetables, soups, stews, and salads, adding seasoning to suit taste.

Makes about 1 cup.

Three nickels will get you on the subway, but garlic will get you a seat.

—Yiddish saying

GARLIC PANCAKES WITH HAM SAUCE

Cooking the garlic until it is soft changes its flavor from pungent to sweet and nut-like, which makes it a pleasant compliment to the smokiness of the ham sauce. Serve for breakfast, brunch, lunch, or even a light supper.

Finalist 1983 Recipe Contest: **John Keith Drummond, San Francisco, CA**

½ pound butter

3 tablespoons rubbed sage

3 large heads fresh garlic

2 cups self-rising flour

2 eggs

2 tablespoons oil

3½ cups milk

9 large cloves fresh garlic, minced

1 pound lean ham, minced

Combine 12 tablespoons (1½ sticks) butter and the sage; reserve. Remove as much outer skin from garlic as possible without piercing the cloves' covering. Place garlic in a saucepan, cover with water, and boil gently about 45 minutes, or until cloves are quite soft. Remove from heat. When cool enough to handle, squeeze each clove to remove cooked garlic by grasping clove at the tip and pulling down toward base. In a mixing bowl, beat garlic with a fork until smooth. Add to the garlic equal amounts (at least 1 cup each) flour, eggs, and oil, and 1½ cups milk to make pancake batter. Add minced garlic to batter and set aside. Melt remaining 4 tablespoons butter and keep warm. Place half the sage butter (6 tablespoons) in a saucepan, add 6 tablespoons flour to make a roux; cook at medium temperature, stirring frequently, to brown. Meanwhile, in a skillet, place 2 tablespoons of remaining sage butter and add ham. Heat through, but do not burn. When roux is nicely browned, add remaining 2 cups milk. Allow to thicken, stirring frequently. Add ham and skillet drippings and mix to make ham sauce. Keep warm. Heat a griddle or a clean skillet and grease lightly with a little bit of the remaining sage butter. Drop batter by spoonfuls onto the griddle to make silver dollar-sized pancakes. Serve with melted butter and ham sauce.

Makes 2 dozen pancakes.

CREPES POULE GARLIC

For extra garlic flavor, be sure to have some garlic oil on hand to add to the crepe batter. Just add a few cloves of peeled fresh garlic to a bottle of vegetable oil a few days before you prepare this recipe.

Recipe Contest entry: **Marty Tielemans, Gilroy, CA**

Veloute Sauce
¹/₃ cup butter

3¹/₂ tablespoons flour

I cup chicken broth

Filling
¹/₄ pound mushrooms, sliced

2 tablespoons butter

I cup cooked chicken chunks

6 cloves fresh garlic, finely
    chopped

2 tablespoons chopped
    green onion

I tablespoon sherry

¹/₂ teaspoon salt

3 dashes Tabasco

¹/₃ cup Veloute Sauce (see
    recipe above)

Crepes
4 eggs

I¹/₂ cups milk

I cup sifted flour

¹/₄ cup sherry

2 teaspoons garlic-
    flavored oil

Dash salt

Dash nutmeg

Topping
I cup Veloute Sauce

¹/₂ cup whipping cream

I beaten egg yolk

¹/₄ cup butter

I cup grated Romano cheese

2 teaspoons paprika

To make the veloute sauce: Melt butter; stir in flour, and cook over medium heat until golden in color. Gradually stir in broth. Cook, stirring, until thick. Set aside.

To make the filling: Brown mushrooms in butter. Add chicken, garlic, onion, sherry, salt, and Tabasco. Mix well. Add Veloute Sauce to moisten.

To make the crepes: Blend all ingredients; cook crepes in a crepe pan or on a hot buttered griddle. Use about 2 tablespoons batter for each crepe.

To make the topping: Place remaining Veloute Sauce in a pan; add cream and stir until smooth. Add eggs and butter. Assemble crepes by placing equal amounts of chicken filling across the center of each crepe and roll up. Place in a shallow baking pan, rolled-side down. Cover with topping; sprinkle with cheese and paprika. Broil until golden brown.

Makes about 12 crepes.

GARLIC CHIP COOKIES

Cookies made with garlic? Why not? Everyone who tasted them agreed they were delicious and would even be better with more garlic.

Finalist 1984 Recipe Contest: **Michele Sciortino, San Diego, CA**

10 cloves fresh garlic

Boiling water

$^1/_2$ cup maple syrup

1 cup butter, softened

$^3/_4$ cup brown sugar

$^3/_4$ cup sugar

2 eggs

1 teaspoon vanilla

$^1/_2$ teaspoon salt

$2^1/_4$ cups chocolate chips

$^1/_2$ cup chopped nuts

$2^1/_2$ cups flour

1 teaspoon baking soda

Drop garlic cloves into boiling water, about 5 minutes, until tender. Peel and chop garlic and soak in maple syrup for 20 minutes. Meanwhile, cream butter, sugars, eggs, and vanilla together until light and fluffy. Combine flour, baking soda, and salt. Add to cream mixture. Then stir in chocolate chips and nuts. Drain garlic and add to cookie batter. Blend well. Drop by tablespoonfuls onto an ungreased cookie sheet about 2 inches apart. Bake at 375 degrees F. for 8 to 10 minutes, until lightly browned. Remove from oven and cool on racks.

Makes 5 dozen cookies.

HOMEMADE DOG BISCUITS

Nutritious treats for the family dog.

Recipe Contest entry: **G. C. Bemis, Pebble Beach, CA**

3 ½ cups all-purpose flour

2 cups whole-wheat flour

2 cups bran

1 cup rye flour

1 cup grits *or* cornmeal

½ cup nonfat dry milk

1 tablespoon dehydrated minced *or* powdered garlic

4 teaspoons salt (optional)

1 package dry yeast

¼ cup warm water

2 cups tomato juice

Combine all dry ingredients. Dissolve yeast in warm water and add tomato juice. Mix with dry ingredients. Dough should be very stiff. Knead dough about 3 minutes. Roll out on a floured board to ¼- to ½-inch thickness. Cut to desired size with a knife or cookie cutters. Place on an ungreased cookie sheet and bake at 300 degrees F. for 1 hour. Turn off oven. Leave biscuits overnight or at least 4 hours to harden.

Makes about 7 dozen biscuits.

Garlic, very versatile, puts zing in bland dishes.

—Los Angeles Times

Index